Off-road routes

First published 1996 by

Ordnance Survey   and   Philip's, an imprint of
Romsey Road   Reed Books
Maybush   Michelin House
Southampton   81 Fulham Road
SO16 4GU   London SW3 6RB

Text and compilation
Copyright © Reed International Books Ltd 1996
Maps Copyright © Crown Copyright 1996
First edition 1996

A catalogue record for this atlas is available from the British Library

ISBN 0 600 58847 5
(Ordnance Survey ISBN 0 319 00785 5)

Printed in Spain

Acknowledgments
AA Photo Library *49, 115, 119, 131* • Nick Cotton *138* • Derek Forss *19, 55, 79, 85, 103, 122* • Molyneux Associates / Colin Molyneux *111* • David Tarn *25, 31, 37, 42, 61, 66, 73, 91, 96, 106, 135* • Yorkshire & Humberside Tourist Board *back cover, 127*
• edited by Melissa Arnison-Newgass • designed by James Hughes
• picture research by Jenny Faithfull • production by Claudette Morris

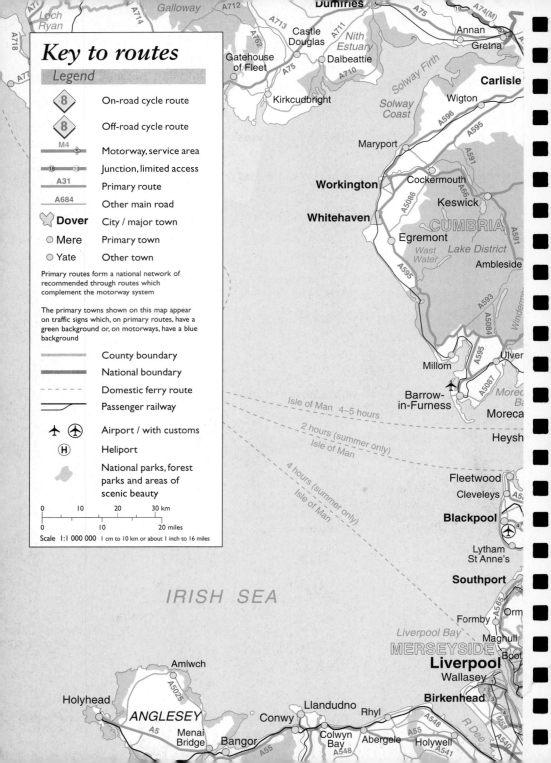

Key to routes

Legend

⑧	On-road cycle route
⑧	Off-road cycle route
M4 ⓢ	Motorway, service area
18 — 19	Junction, limited access
A31	Primary route
A684	Other main road
Dover	City / major town
○ Mere	Primary town
○ Yate	Other town

Primary routes form a national network of recommended through routes which complement the motorway system

The primary towns shown on this map appear on traffic signs which, on primary routes, have a green background or, on motorways, have a blue background

	County boundary
	National boundary
- - -	Domestic ferry route
	Passenger railway
✈ ✈	Airport / with customs
Ⓗ	Heliport
	National parks, forest parks and areas of scenic beauty

Scale 1:1 000 000 1 cm to 10 km or about 1 inch to 16 miles

0   10   20   30 km
0   10   20 miles

Dumfries
Galloway
A712
A74(M)
Annan
A75
Castle Douglas
A713
A711
A762
Gretna
Gatehouse of Fleet
Dalbeattie
A75
Nith Estuary
Carlisle
A710
Solway Firth
Kirkcudbright
Wigton
A596
Solway Coast
Maryport
A595
A591
Cockermouth
Workington
A5086
A66
Keswick
Whitehaven
CUMBRIA
A591
Egremont
Wast Water
Lake District
Ambleside
A595
A593
Windermere
A5084
A595
Millom
Ulverston
A5087
Barrow-in-Furness
Morecambe Bay
Morecambe
Isle of Man 4–5 hours
Heysham
2 hours (summer only)
Isle of Man
Fleetwood
4 hours (summer only)
Isle of Man
Cleveleys
A585
Blackpool
Lytham St Anne's
Southport
IRISH SEA
Formby
Orm
Liverpool Bay
A565
Maghull
MERSEYSIDE
Boot
Liverpool
Wallasey
Amlwch
A5025
Birkenhead
Holyhead
ANGLESEY
Llandudno
Rhyl
R Dee
A5
Menai Bridge
Conwy
Colwyn Bay
Abergele
Holywell
A548
Bangor
A55
A548
A541

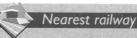

Nearest railway

Horton in Ribblesdale

Refreshments

Golden Lion PH 🍺, *Crown PH, cafe* **Horton**
George PH 🍺🍺, **Hubberholme** *(8 km
(5 miles) off the route, along the valley road
east of instruction 7)*

Places of interest

Ling Hill *3/4*
This fragment of Pennine Gorge woodland
has survived due to its
protection from grazing animals.
The woods contain an attractive
mixture of trees and shrubs such
as Ash and Bird Cherry with a
wide variety of wild flowers

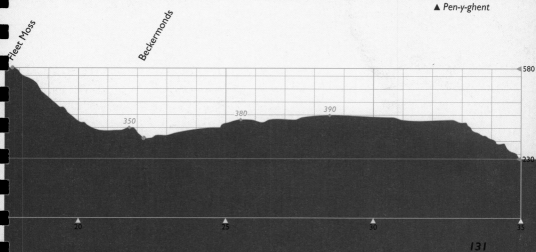

▲ Pen-y-ghent

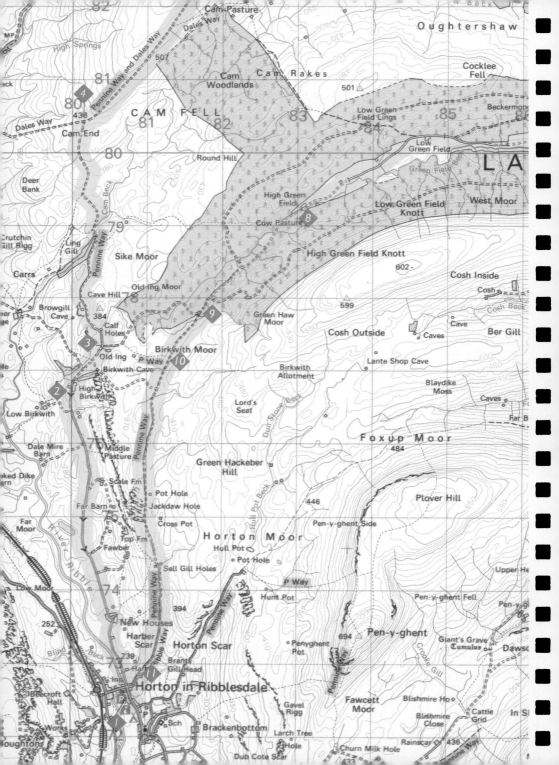

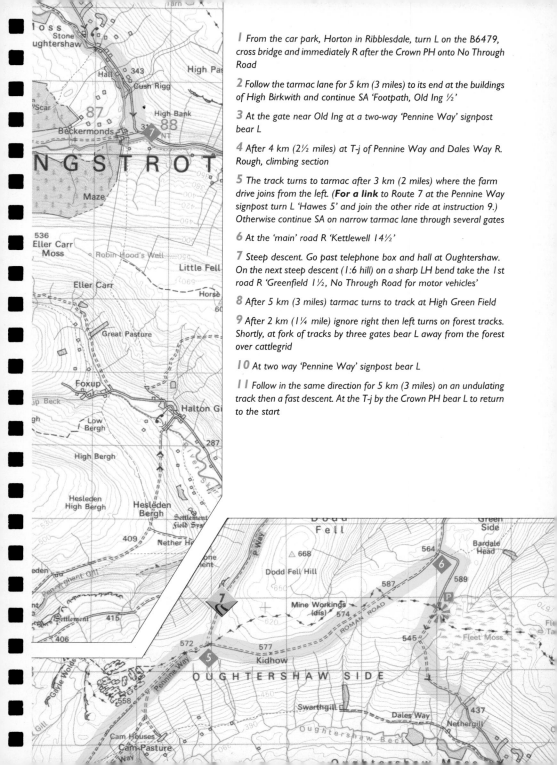

1 *From the car park, Horton in Ribblesdale, turn L on the B6479, cross bridge and immediately R after the Crown PH onto No Through Road*

2 Follow the tarmac lane for 5 km (3 miles) to its end at the buildings of High Birkwith and continue SA 'Footpath, Old Ing ½'

3 At the gate near Old Ing at a two-way 'Pennine Way' signpost bear L

4 After 4 km (2½ miles) at T-j of Pennine Way and Dales Way R. Rough, climbing section

5 The track turns to tarmac after 3 km (2 miles) where the farm drive joins from the left. (**For a link** to Route 7 at the Pennine Way signpost turn L 'Hawes 5' and join the other ride at instruction 9.) Otherwise continue SA on narrow tarmac lane through several gates

6 At the 'main' road R 'Kettlewell 14½'

7 Steep descent. Go past telephone box and hall at Oughtershaw. On the next steep descent (1:6 hill) on a sharp LH bend take the 1st road R 'Greenfield 1½, No Through Road for motor vehicles'

8 After 5 km (3 miles) tarmac turns to track at High Green Field

9 After 2 km (1¼ mile) ignore right then left turns on forest tracks. Shortly, at fork of tracks by three gates bear L away from the forest over cattlegrid

10 At two way 'Pennine Way' signpost bear L

11 Follow in the same direction for 5 km (3 miles) on an undulating track then a fast descent. At the T-j by the Crown PH bear L to return to the start

9 East from Settle to Malham Cove

Malham Cove is one of the most spectacular sights of the Yorkshire Dales and there can be few more exhilarating ways of getting there from Settle than the one described below. All routes leading east from Settle face a steep climb, in this case on a tarmac lane, turning into a good stone track. There is a delightful section along Stockdale. The track steepens and there follows a well-drained, grassy section ending with a lovely descent to the road above Malham Cove. The 3-km (2-mile) section of track on the moorland returning over Gorbeck should only be attempted in summer and autumn and may well be rough or muddy at any time of the year. A road alternative is also described. The track does improve and from here back to the start is one long descent.

Start

Tourist Information Centre, Settle

P Follow signs

Distance and grade

19 km (12 miles) or 27 km (17 miles) with circuit of Malham Tarn

Strenuous

Terrain

Fine stone and well-drained grass track on outward leg: rough 3-km (2-mile) section on return leg (or road alternative). Two climbs: 350 m (1150 ft) from the start to the top of Kirkby Fell (very steep at the start): 110 m (360 ft) from the road above Malham Cove west to the highpoint on the moorland. Lowest point – 160 m (525 ft)

▶ Malham Cove

Refreshments

Royal Oak PH 🍴*, plenty of choice in* **Settle**
Lister Arms 🍴🍴*, plenty of choice in* **Malham**
(just off the route at instruction 8)

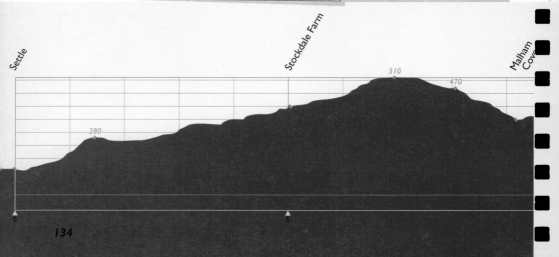

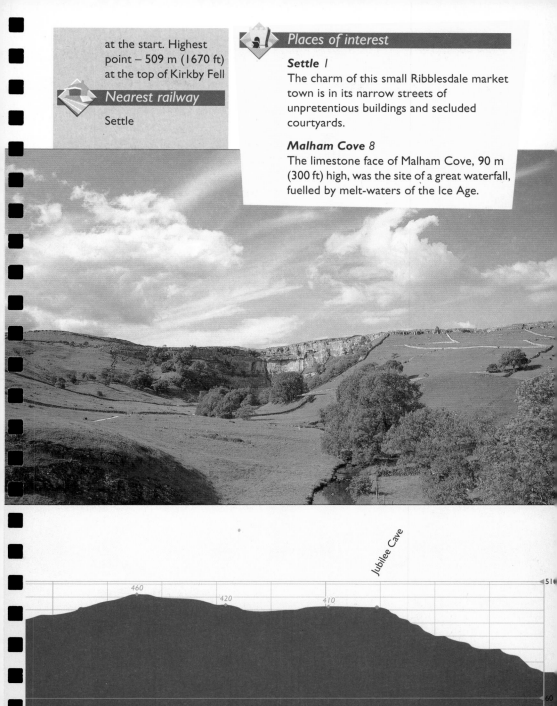

at the start. Highest
point – 509 m (1670 ft)
at the top of Kirkby Fell

Nearest railway

Settle

Places of interest

Settle 1
The charm of this small Ribblesdale market
town is in its narrow streets of
unpretentious buildings and secluded
courtyards.

Malham Cove 8
The limestone face of Malham Cove, 90 m
(300 ft) high, was the site of a great waterfall,
fuelled by melt-waters of the Ice Age.

Jubilee Cave

460
420
410

51

60

10
15
19

135

1 With your back to the Tourist Information Centre L then at T-j R onto High Street past the Talbot PH. At the next T-j L onto Victoria Street 'Kirby Malham 5¼, Airton 6¼'

2 Cobbled secton. Short steep climb. At the '7 ft 6 in width limit' sign at the end of the village turn R by triangle of grass onto No Through Road

3 At a fork of tracks after 2 km (1¼ miles) as the gradient eases after a tough climb bear L onto walled track 'Bridleway, High Hill Lane ½'

4 At T-j with road R then 1st L 'Bridleway, Malham 4, Stockdale'

5 At fork of tracks at the end of the tarmac bear L through wooden gate onto rougher track 'Bridleway, Malham 3½'

6 The rough stone track ends at the top of a steep climb and becomes an obvious, firm, grassy track. Continue in the same direction over the brow of the hill

7 At a signpost continue SA 'Bridleway, Cove Road 1¼'

8 Superb views of Malham Tarn, Malham Cove and the whole limestone plateau. At T-j with road L

9 At the cattle grid and Malham Tarn Estate sign turn L uphill through wooden gate – see on-road alternative

Take care not to mistake the faded yellow line of the national park boundary for the solid yellow line of the route

to wet weather/winter section. (**Or** for a circuit of Malham Tarn, cross cattle grid, then shortly bear R by signpost onto grassy track 'Malham Tarn ¾ mile')

10 After 1 km at fork of tracks by gateway and stonewall with yellow spot bear R (in effect SA) The track deteriorates but remains fairly visible

11 The track improves and soon becomes stone-based

12 At T-j with road turn L through gate onto track 'Bridleway, Settle 1¼'

13 Follow through several fields, finishing with an enclosed stone track. At T-j with road L then bear R to return to square

Alternative route

For use in winter or wet weather

A At the cattle grid go SA. At X-roads L 'Langcliffe 5, Settle 5'. At T-j immediately after cattle grid bear L (in effect SA) 'Langcliffe 3¾, Settle 4¾'

B Follow the road round to the L (your right of way)

C After 5 km (3½ miles) at T-j with the B6479 at the bottom of a steep descent L 'Settle 1', then shortly 1st L onto No Through Road to return to the centre of Settle

10 ◆ Along the Nidderdale Way between two reservoirs

The course of the route runs along Nidderdale linking Gouthwaite and Scar House reservoirs via sections of the

Start

The bus shelter/lay-by near Wath, 3 km (2 miles) north of Pateley Bridge along Nidderdale

P As above

Distance and grade

35 km (22 miles)

Strenuous

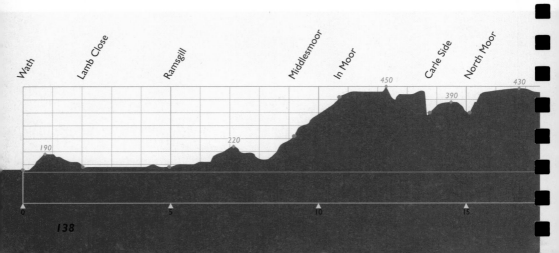

Terrain

Fine stone tracks through valley farmland and heather-clad moorland. Four main climbs: 75 m (250 ft) at the start; 80 m (265 ft) from Ramsgill to High Blayshaw; 250 m (820 ft) from crossing How Stean Beck to the highpoint, south of Scar House Reservoir; 120 m (395 ft) from the reservoir up onto Brown Ridge. Lowest point – 125 m (410 ft) at the start. Highest point – 450 m (1480 ft) on Brown Ridge, north of the River Nidd

Nearest railway

Knaresborough, 24 km (15 miles) southeast of Pateley Bridge

◀ *Alongside Gouthwaite Reservoir*

Nidderdale Way and fine stone tracks over the moorland plateau. The ride immediately leaves the valley road at Wath, climbing steeply through woodland and up onto a delightful track alongside Gouthwaite Reservoir. Moving from the east to west side of the valley, the ride now follows the Nidderdale Way through predominantly pasture land as far as Middlemoor beyond which the moorland section begins. A technical descent drops you at Scar House Reservoir before a climb through the heather. A long, undulating track over the top of the moor leads on to the lane that links Nidderdale to Masham. From here unclassified roads drop gently then more steeply on a short, rubbly section down to Bouthwaite and a return along the valley to the start.

Refreshments

Sportsmans Arms 🍴🍴, **Wath**
Yorke Arms PH 🍴🍴, **Ramsgill**
The following are just off the route:
Crown PH, Royal Oak PH, tea shops in **Pateley Bridge**
Crown Inn, How Steam Gorge Cafe,
Lofthouse

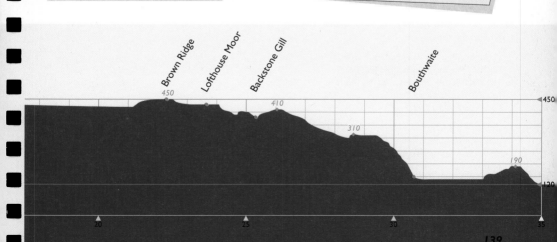

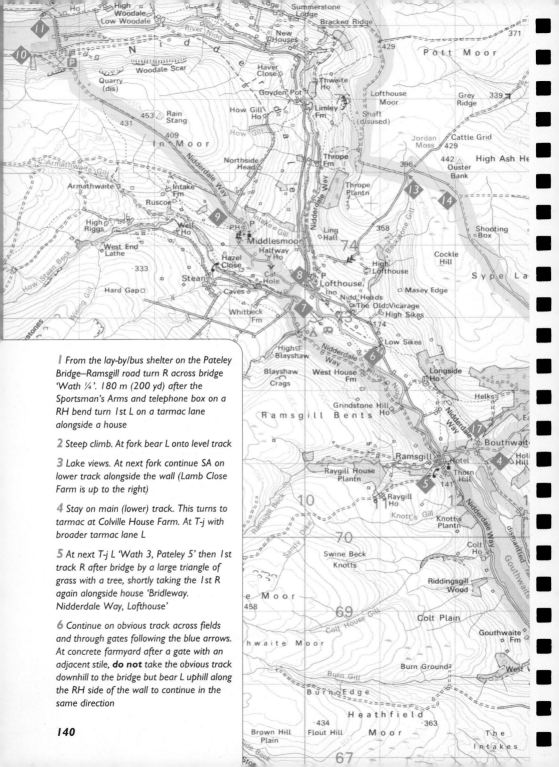

1 *From the lay-by/bus shelter on the Pateley Bridge–Ramsgill road turn R across bridge 'Wath ¼'. 180 m (200 yd) after the Sportsman's Arms and telephone box on a RH bend turn 1st L on a tarmac lane alongside a house*

2 *Steep climb. At fork bear L onto level track*

3 *Lake views. At next fork continue SA on lower track alongside the wall (Lamb Close Farm is up to the right)*

4 *Stay on main (lower) track. This turns to tarmac at Colville House Farm. At T-j with broader tarmac lane L*

5 *At next T-j L 'Wath 3, Pateley 5' then 1st track R after bridge by a large triangle of grass with a tree, shortly taking the 1st R again alongside house 'Bridleway. Nidderdale Way, Lofthouse'*

6 *Continue on obvious track across fields and through gates following the blue arrows. At concrete farmyard after a gate with an adjacent stile, **do not** take the obvious track downhill to the bridge but bear L uphill along the RH side of the wall to continue in the same direction*

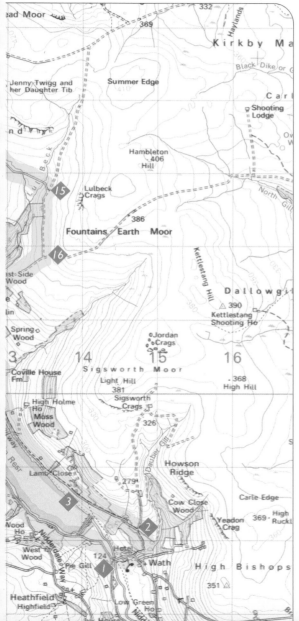

7 At T-j of tracks by houses turn R steeply downhill towards caravan site. Follow the track and Nidderdale Way signs round to the L. At tarmac turn R over bridge

8 At T-j L 'Middlesmoor only'

9 Climb steeply into Middlesmoor and go past the Crown Inn. Continue in the same direction as tarmac turns to track

10 Long steady climb then fast technical descent. At T-j with tarmac R then after 365 m (400 yd) L to cross dam 'Nidderdale Way'

11 At the end of dam bear L uphill on broad cobblestone track for 140 m (150 yd) then turn R sharply back on yourself 'Nidderdale Way'

12 Climb then descend into steep gully. Cross stream via wooden bridge. **Easy to miss**. Climb steeply. Shortly after the gradient eases, with a small square, stone building 365 m (400 yd) ahead bear L towards mining spoil heap then swing R on a level path towards gate in the wall ahead

13 Follow the main, undulating, stone-based track for 6 km (4 miles). At T-j with road L then after 90 m (100 yd) R 'Unsuitable for motors'

14 After 1 km fork R

15 After 3 km (2 miles) descend to cross stone bridge. Climb then bear R through gate towards wood

16 At T-j R 'Unsuitable for motors'

17 At bottom of steep (at times stony) descent, you have a choice – turn L on 'Bridleway to Wath' to repeat the outward route **or** go SA to road then at T-j L 'Wath 3, Pateley Bridge 5' . Both routes lead back to the start

Cycle Cycle Cycle
TOURS TOURS TOURS

The Ordnance Survey Cycle Tours series

Around Birmingham
Around London
Avon, Somerset & Wiltshire
Berks, Bucks & Oxfordshire
Cornwall & Devon
Cumbria & the Lakes
Dorset, Hampshire & Isle of Wight
East Anglia – South
Gloucestershire and Hereford & Worcester
Kent, Surrey & Sussex
Peak District
Southern Scotland
South, West and Mid-Wales
Yorkshire Dales

*T*he whole series is available from all good bookshops or by mail order direct from the publisher. Payment can be made by credit card or cheque/postal order in the following ways

By phone

Phone through your order on our special *Credit Card Hotline* on *01933 414000*. Speak to our customer service team during office hours (9am to 5pm) or leave a message on the answer machine, quoting your full credit card number plus expiry date, your full name and address and reference T606N731

By post

Simply fill out the order form opposite and send it to:
Cash Sales Department, Reed Book Services, PO Box 5, Rushden, Northants, NN10 6YX

Cycle Cycle Cycle
TOURS TOURS TOURS

I wish to order the following titles

	Price	Quantity	Total
Around Birmingham ISBN 0 600 58623 5	£9.99		
Around London ISBN 0 600 58845 9	£9.99		
Avon, Somerset & Wiltshire ISBN 0 600 58664 2	£9.99		
Berks, Bucks & Oxfordshire ISBN 0 600 58156 X	£9.99		
Cornwall & Devon ISBN 0 600 58124 1	£9.99		
Cumbria & the Lakes ISBN 0 600 58126 8	£9.99		
Dorset, Hampshire & Isle of Wight ISBN 0 600 58667 7	£9.99		
East Anglia – South ISBN 0 600 58125 X	£9.99		
Gloucestershire and Hereford & Worcester ISBN 0 600 58665 0	£9.99		
Kent, Surrey & Sussex ISBN 0 600 58666 9	£9.99		
Peak District ISBN 0 600 58889 0	£9.99		
Southern Scotland ISBN 0 600 58624 3	£9.99		
South, West and Mid-Wales ISBN 0 600 58846 7	£9.99		
Yorkshire Dales ISBN 0 600 58847 5	£9.99		

Postage and packing free   Grand total [   ]

Name_____ (block capitals)

Address_____

_____ Postcode

I enclose a cheque/postal order for £ [   ] made payable to **Reed Book Services Ltd**

or please debit my ☐ Access ☐ Visa ☐ American Express ☐ Diners account

number [   ] [   ] [   ] [   ]

by £ [   ] expiry date [ ] [ ] [ ] _____ Signature

Quick reference chart

Route	Page	Distance (kilometres)	Grade (easy/moderate/strenuous)	Links with other routes[1]	Tourist information centres[2]
On-road routes					
1 From Richmond over The Stang into Arkengarthdale	18	50	🚲🚲🚲🚲🚲	2,3	Richmond 01748 850252
2 Tan Hill and Swaledale, west of Reeth	24	43	🚲🚲🚲🚲	1,3	Richmond 01748 850252
3 Wensleydale and Swaledale, north of Aysgarth	30	56	🚲🚲🚲🚲🚲	1,2,4	Hawes 01969 667450
4 From Aysgarth to Hubberholme	36	48	🚲🚲🚲🚲🚲	3,5,8	Hawes 01969 667450
5 From Aysgarth to Kettlewell	42	58	🚲🚲🚲🚲🚲	3,4, 10,13	Leyburn 01969 23069
6 From Pateley Bridge to Masham, returning along Nidderdale	48	45	🚲🚲🚲🚲🚲	7	Pateley Bridge 01423 711147
7 An easy ride from Ripon to Bedale	54	51	🚲	6	Ripon 01765 604625
8 A circuit around Whernside	60	45	🚲🚲🚲🚲	3,4,9	Ingleton 015242 41049
9 West from Settle to Ingleton and Wray	66	56	🚲🚲🚲	8,11	Settle 01729 825192
10 From Settle to Malham and along Littondale	72	48	🚲🚲🚲🚲🚲	5,9, 13	Settle 01729 825192
11 Gisburn Forest and Bolton-by-Bowland	78	58	🚲🚲🚲🚲🚲	10,12	Settle 01729 825192
12 Slaidburn and the Trough of Bowland	84	56	🚲🚲🚲🚲	11	Clitheroe 01200 25566
13 From Skipton to Grassington	90	45	🚲🚲🚲	14	Skipton 01756 792809
14 From Skipton to Ilkley Moor and Bolton Abbey	96	42	🚲🚲🚲	5,10, 13	Skipton 01756 792809

Route	Page	Distance (kilometres)	Grade (easy/moderate/strenuous)	Links with other routes[1]	Tourist information centres[2]

Off-road routes

Route	Page	Distance (kilometres)	Grade	Links with other routes[1]	Tourist information centres[2]
1 Along the River Swale to Keld	102	21	🚲🚲🚲🚲	2	Hawes 01969 667450
2 From Feetham through mining ruins on Melbecks Moor	106	17	🚲🚲🚲🚲🚲	1,3,4,5	Hawes 01969 667450
3 From Reeth, over Marrick Moor and Hurst Moor	110	21	🚲🚲🚲🚲	2,4	Leyburn 01969 23069
4 Along Swaledale and over Apedale	114	22	🚲🚲🚲🚲	2,3,5	Leyburn 01969 23069
5 North from Castle Bolton and up over The Fleak	118	24	🚲🚲🚲🚲🚲	2,4,6,7	Leyburn 01969 23069
6 From Aysgarth along Wensleydale and onto Stake Allotments	122	24	🚲🚲🚲🚲	5,7	Leyburn 01969 23069
7 Down the Pennine Way south of Hawes	126	32	🚲🚲🚲🚲🚲	5,6,8	Hawes 01969 667450
8 The Pennine Way, north of Horton in Ribblesdale	130	35	🚲🚲🚲🚲	7	Settle 01729 825192
9 East from Settle to Malham Cove	134	19	🚲🚲🚲🚲🚲		Settle 01729 825192
10 Along the Nidderdale Way between two reservoirs	138	35	🚲🚲🚲🚲🚲		Pateley Bridge 01423 711147

[1] **Links with other routes** Use this information to create a more strenuous ride or if you are planning to do more than one ride in a day or on a weekend or over a few days. The rides do not necessarily join: there may be a distance of up to three miles between the closest points. Several rides are in pairs, sharing the same starting point, which may be a good place to base yourself for a weekend.

[2] **Tourist Information Centres** You can contact them for details about accommodation. If they cannot help, there are many books that recommend places to stay. If nothing is listed for the place where you want to stay, try phoning the post office or the pub in the village to see if they can suggest somewhere.

Yorkshire Dales

*T*he geological structure of dales dictates a road network that makes full use of the gentle gradients along the valley floors while the dales are connected by narrow lanes that rise steeply up the hillsides and drop just as steeply down the other side.

It is very easy to link one route to another in this collection and the on-road routes have been grouped into four clusters: routes 1–5 explore Arkengarthdale, Swaledale and Wensleydale; routes 6 and 7 cover the area between Ripon and Pateley Bridge; routes 8–12 are based on Settle. The final two routes run north and east from Skipton. Between them the rides offer the possibility of anything from a day out to a week's touring or more. The off-road rides are even more closely spaced with all but three rides based in Swaledale and Wensleydale.

Few of the rides in this book are easy. Some of the road gradients are as steep as 1 in 4 but they only represent a small part of each ride. Walking up the steepest section of a climb may only add 15–20 minutes to a ride lasting 3–4 hours, will rest one set of muscles and not drain your reserves so quickly.

The Yorkshire Dales National Park authority is keen to promote a responsible attitude towards the sustainable use of the off-road tracks, with this in mind every effort has been made to indicate road alternatives to stretches that may be soft or muddy from late autumn to late spring and after prolonged rain at any time of year. Please follow these alternatives rather than making any existing problem worse and in the depths of winter give serious consideration to trying one of the on-road rides along the quiet lanes as a better option than the off-road rides.

Abbreviations and instructions

Instructions are given as concisely as possible to make them easy to follow while you are cycling. Remember to read one or two instructions ahead so that you do not miss a turning. This is most likely to occur when you have to turn off a road on which you have been riding for a fairly long distance and these junctions are marked **Easy to miss** to warn you.

If there appears to be a contradiction between the instructions and what you actually see, always refer to the map. There are many reasons why over the course of a few years instructions will need updating as new roads are built and priorities and signposts change.

If giving instructions for road routes is at times difficult, doing so for off-road routes can often be almost impossible, particularly when the route passes through woodland. With few signposts and buildings by which to orientate yourself, more attention is paid to other features, such as gradient and surface. Most of these routes have been explored between late spring and early autumn and the countryside changes its appearance very dramatically in winter. If in doubt, consult your map and check your compass to see that you are heading in the right direction.

Where I have encountered mud I have mentioned it, but this may change, not only from summer to winter but also from dry to wet weather, at any time during the year. At times you may have to retrace your steps and find a road alternative.

Some routes have small sections that follow footpaths. The instructions will highlight these sections where you must get off and push your bike. You may only ride on bridleways and by-ways so be careful if you stray from the given routes.

Directions	
L	left
LH	left-hand
RH	right-hand
SA	straight ahead or straight across
bear L or R	make less than a 90-degree (right-angle) turn at a fork in the road or track or at a sharp bend so that your course appears to be straight ahead; this is often written as in effect SA
sharp L or R turn	is more acute than 90 degrees
sharp R/L back on yourself	an almost U-turn
sharp LH/RH bend	a 90-degree bend
R then L or R	the second turning is visible then immediately L from the first
R then 1st L	the second turning may be some distance from the first; the distance may also be indicated: R, then after 1 mile L

Junctions

T-j	T-junction, a junction where you have to give way
X-roads	crossroads, a junction where you may or may not have to give way
offset X-roads	the four roads are not in the form of a perfect cross and you will have to turn left then right, or vice versa, to continue the route

Signs

'Placename 2'	words in quotation marks are those that appear on signposts; the numbers indicate distance in miles unless stated otherwise
NS	not signposted
trig point	a trigonometrical station

Instructions

An example of an easy instruction is:

4 At the T-j at the end of Smith Road by the White Swan PH R on Brown Street 'Greentown 2, Redville 3'.

There is more information in this instruction than you would normally need, but things do change: pubs may close down and signs may be replaced, removed or vandalized.

An example of a difficult instruction is:

8 Shortly after the brow of the hill, soon after passing a telephone box on the right next L (NS).

As you can see, there is no T-junction to halt you in your tracks, no signpost indicating where the left turn will take you, so you need to have your wits about you in order not to miss the turning.

Fact boxes

The introduction to each route includes a fact box giving useful information:

Start

This is the suggested start point coinciding with instruction 1 on the map. There is no reason why you should not start at another point if you prefer.

Distance and grade

The distance is, of course, that from the beginning to the end of the route. If you wish to shorten the ride, however, the maps enable you to do so.

The number of drinks bottles indicates the grade:

Easy
Moderate
Strenuous

Page diagrams

The on-road routes usually occupy four pages of mapping each. The page diagrams on the introductory pages show how the map pages have been laid out, how they overlap and if any inset maps have been used.

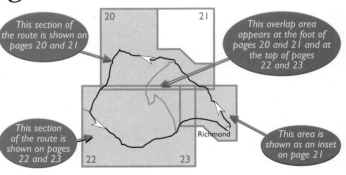

This section of the route is shown on pages 20 and 21

This overlap area appears at the foot of pages 20 and 21 and at the top of pages 22 and 23

This section of the route is shown on pages 22 and 23

This area is shown as an inset on page 21

The grade is based on the amount of climbing involved.

Remember that conditions may vary dramatically with the weather and seasons, especially along off-road sections

Terrain

This brief description of the terrain may be read in conjunction with the cross-profile diagram at the foot of the page to help you to plan your journey.

Nearest railway

This is the distance to the nearest station from the closest point on the route, not necessarily from the start. Before starting out you should check with British Rail for local restrictions regarding the carrying of bicycles.
(See page 15)

Refreshments

Pubs and teashops on or near the route are listed. The tankard symbols indicate pubs particularly liked by the author

Before you go

Preparing yourself

Fitness
✲ Cycling uses muscles in a different way from walking or running, so if you are beginning or returning to it after a long absence you will need time to train your muscles and become accustomed to sitting on a saddle for a few hours. Build up your fitness and stamina gradually and make sure you are using a bicycle that is the right size for you and suits your needs.

Equipment
✲ Attach the following items to the bike: bell, pump, light-brackets and lights, lock-holder and lock, rack and panniers or elastic straps for securing things to the rack, map holder. Unless it is the middle of summer and the weather is guaranteed to be fine, you will need to carry extra clothes, particularly a waterproof, with you, and it is well worth investing in a rack for this purpose.

✲ Wearing a small pouch around your waist is the easiest and safest way of carrying small tools and personal equipment. The basics are: Allen keys to fit the various Allen bolts on your bike, chainlink extractor, puncture repair kit, reversible screwdriver (slot and crosshead), small adjustable spanner, spare inner tube, tyre levers (not always necessary with mountain bike tyres), coins and a phonecard for food and telephone calls, compass.

✲ Additional tools for extended touring: bottom bracket extractor, cone spanners, freewheel extractor, headset spanners, lubricant, socket spanner for pedals, spare cables, spoke-key.

Clothing
✲ What you wear when you are cycling should be comfortable, allowing you, and most especially your legs, to move freely. It should also be practical, so that it will keep you warm and dry if and when the weather changes.

✲ *Feet* You can cycle in just about any sort of footwear, but bear in mind that the chain has oil on it, so do not use your very best shoes. Leather tennis shoes or something similar, with a smooth sole to slip into the pedal and toe clip are probably adequate until you buy specialist cycling shoes, which have stiffer soles and are sometimes designed for use with specialist pedals.

✲ *Legs* Cycling shorts or padded cycling underwear worn under everyday clothing make long rides much more comfortable. Avoid tight, non-stretch trousers, which are very uncomfortable for cycling and will sap your energy, as they restrict the movement of your legs; baggy tracksuit bottoms, which can get caught in the chain and will sag around your ankles if they get wet. Almost anything else will do, though a pair of stretch leggings is probably best.

Upper body What you wear should be long enough to cover your lower back when you are leaning forward and, ideally, should have zips or buttons that you can adjust to regulate your temperature. Several thin layers are better than one thick layer.

Head A helmet may protect your head in a fall.

Wet weather A waterproof, windproof top is essential if it looks like rain. A dustbin bag would be better than nothing but obviously a breathable waterproof material is best.

Cold weather A hat that covers your ears, a scarf around your neck, a pair of warm gloves and a thermal top and bottom combined with what you would normally wear cycling should cover almost all conditions.

Night and poor light Wearing light-coloured clothes or reflective strips is almost as important as having lights on your bike. Reflective bands worn around the ankles are particularly effective in making you visible to motorists.

Preparing your bicycle

You may not be a bicycle maintenance expert, but you should make sure that your bike is roadworthy before you begin a ride.

If you are planning to ride in soft, off-road conditions, fit fat, knobbly tyres. If you are using the bike around town or on a road route, fit narrower, smoother tyres.

Check the tyres for punctures or damage and repair or replace if necessary or if you are in any doubt. Keep tyres inflated hard (recommended pressures are on the side wall of the tyre) for mainly on-road riding. You do not need to inflate tyres as hard for off-road use; slightly softer tyres give some cushioning and get better traction in muddy conditions.

Ensure that the brakes work efficiently. Replace worn cables and brake blocks.

The bike should glide along silently. Tighten and adjust any part that is loose or rubbing against a moving part. Using a good-quality bike oil lubricate the hubs, bottom bracket, pedals where they join the cranks, chain and gear-changing mechanism from both sides. If the bike still makes grating noises, replace the bearings.

Adjust the saddle properly. The saddle height should ensure that your legs are working efficiently: too low and your knees will ache; too high and your hips will be rocking in order for your feet to reach the pedals. Some women find the average bike saddle uncomfortable because the female pelvis is a different shape from the male pelvis and needs a broader saddle for support. Some manufacturers make saddles especially for women.

Cross-profiles

The introduction to each route includes a cross-profile diagram. The blue grid indicates 1-kilometre horizontal intervals and 50-metre vertical intervals

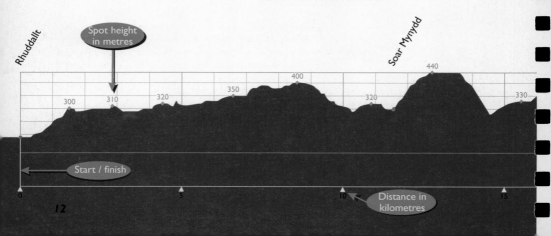

Rhuddallt

Spot height in metres

Soar Mynydd

440

400

350

320

310

300

320

330

Start / finish

0   5   10   Distance in kilometres   15

Tips for touring

The law

Engeland and Wales have 120 000 miles of rights of way, but under the Wildlife and Countryside Act of 1968 you are allowed to cycle on only about 10 percent of them, namely on bridleways, by-ways open to all traffic (BOATS) and roads used as public paths (RUPPS).

The other 90 percent of rights of way are footpaths, where you may walk and usually push your bike, but not ride it. Local bylaws sometimes prohibit the pushing of bicycles along footpaths and although all the paths in this book have been checked, bylaws do sometimes change.

⚙ You are not allowed to ride where there is no right of way. If you lose the route and find yourself in conflict with a landowner, stay calm and courteous, make a note of exactly where you are and then contact the Rights of Way Department of the local authority. It has copies of definitive maps and will take up the matter on your behalf if you are in the right.

Cycling techniques

If you are not used to cycling more than a few miles at a stretch, you may find initially that touring is tiring. There are ways of conserving your energy, however:

⚙ Do not struggle in a difficult gear if you have an easier one. Let the gears help you up the hills. No matter how many gears a bike has, however, ultimately it is leg power that you need to get you up a hill. You may decide to get off and walk uphill with your bike to rest your muscles.

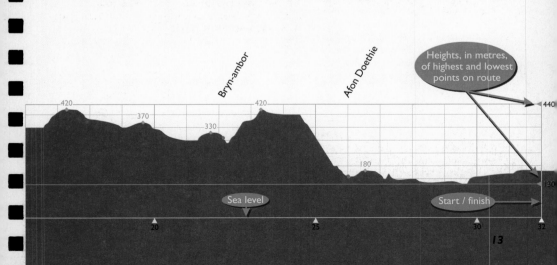

- You can save a lot of energy on the road by following close behind a stronger rider in his or her slipstream, but do not try this offroad. All the routes are circular, so you can start at any point and follow the instructions until you return to it. This is useful when there is a strong wind, as you can alter the route to go into the wind at the start of the ride, when you are fresh, and have the wind behind you on the return, when you are more tired.

- The main difference in technique between on-road and off-road cycling lies in getting your weight balanced correctly. When going down steep off-road sections, lower the saddle, keep the pedals level, stand up out of the saddle to let your legs absorb the bumps and keep your weight over the rear wheel. Control is paramount: keep your eyes on what lies ahead.

Traffic

The rides in this book are designed to minimize time spent on busy roads, but you will inevitably encounter some traffic. The most effective way to avoid an accident with a motor vehicle is to be highly aware of what is going on around you and to ensure that other road users are aware of you.

- Ride confidently.

- Indicate clearly to other road users what you intend to do, particularly when turning right. Look behind you, wait for a gap in the traffic, indicate, then turn. If you have to turn right off a busy road or on a difficult bend, pull in and wait for a gap in the traffic or go past the turning to a point where you have a clear view of the traffic in both directions, then cross and return to the turning.

- Use your lights and wear reflective clothing at night and in poor light.

- Do not ride two-abreast if there is a vehicle behind you. Let it pass. If it cannot easily overtake you because the road is narrow, look for a passing place or a gate entrance and pull in to let it pass.

Maintenance

Mountain bikes are generally stronger than road bikes, but any bike can suffer. To prevent damage as far as possible:

- Watch out for holes and obstacles.

- Clean off mud and lubricate moving parts regularly.

- Replace worn parts, particularly brake blocks.

Riders also need maintenance:

- Eat before you get hungry, drink before you get thirsty. Dried fruit, nuts and chocolate take up little space and provide lots of energy.

- Carry a water bottle and keep it filled, especially on hot days. Tea, water and well-diluted soft drinks are the best thirst-quenchers.

Breakdowns

The most likely breakdown to occur is a puncture.

- Always carry a pump.

- Take a spare inner tube so that you can leave the puncture repair until later.

- Make sure you know how to remove a wheel. This may require an adjustable spanner or, in many cases, no tool at all, as many bikes now have wheels with quick-release skewers that can be loosened by hand.

Security

Where you park your bike, what you lock it with and to are important in protecting it from being stolen.

- Buy the best lock you can afford.

- Lock your bike to something immovable in a well-lit public place.

- Locking two bikes together is better than locking them individually.

- Use a chain with a lock to secure the wheels and saddle to the frame. Keep a note of the frame number and other details, and insure, photograph and code the bike.

Transporting your bike

There are three ways of getting you and your bike to the start of a ride:

Cycle to the start or to a point along a route near your home.

Take the train. Always check in advance that you can take the bike on the train. Some trains allow only up to two bikes and you may need to make a reservation and pay a flat fee however long the journey. Always label your bike showing your name and destination station.

Travel by motor vehicle. You can carry the bikes:

- Inside the vehicle. With the advent of quick release mechanisms on both wheels and the seatpost, which allow a quick dismantling of the bike, it is possible to fit a bike in even quite small cars. It is unwise to stack one bike on top of another unless you have a thick blanket separating them to prevent scratching or worse damage. If you are standing them up in a van, make sure they are secured so they cannot slide around.

- On top of the vehicle. The advantages of this method are that the bikes are completely out of the way and are not resting against each other, you can get at the boot or hatch easily and the bikes do not obscure the number plate or rear lights and indicators. The disadvantages are that you use up more fuel, the car can feel uncomfortable in a crosswind and you have to be reasonably tall and strong to get the bikes on and off the roof.

- On a rack that attaches to the rear of the vehicle. The advantages are that the rack is easily and quickly assembled and disassembled, fuel consumption is better and anyone can lift the bikes on and off. The disadvantages are that you will need to invest in a separate board carrying the number plate and rear lights if they are obstructed by the bikes, you cannot easily get to the boot or hatch once the bikes have been loaded and secured, and the bikes are resting against each other so you must take care that they don't scrape off paint or damage delicate parts.

- Whichever way you carry the bikes on the outside of the vehicle, ensure that you regularly check that they are secure and that straps and fixings that hold them in place have not come loose. If you are leaving the bikes for any length of time, be sure they are secure against theft; if nothing else lock them to each other.

Legend to 1:50 000 maps

Roads and paths

Motorway

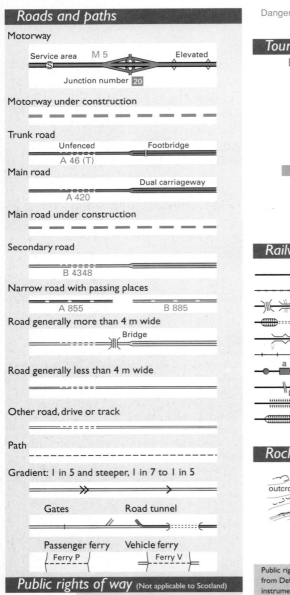

Service area
S
M 5
Elevated
Junction number 20

Motorway under construction

Trunk road

Unfenced — Footbridge

A 46 (T)

Main road

Dual carriageway

A 420

Main road under construction

Secondary road

B 4348

Narrow road with passing places

A 855 — B 885

Road generally more than 4 m wide

Bridge

Road generally less than 4 m wide

Other road, drive or track

Path

Gradient: 1 in 5 and steeper, 1 in 7 to 1 in 5

Gates — Road tunnel

Passenger ferry — Vehicle ferry

Ferry P — Ferry V

Public rights of way (Not applicable to Scotland)

- Footpath
- Bridleway
- Road used as a public footpath
- Byway open to all traffic

Danger Area — Firing and test ranges in the area. Danger! Observe warning notices

Tourist information

- Information centre, all year / seasonal
- Parking
- Picnic site
- Viewpoint
- Camp site
- Caravan site
- Youth hostel
- Selected places of tourist interest
- Public telephone
- Motoring organisation telephone
- Golf course or link
- PC — Public convenience (in rural areas)

Railways

- Track: multiple or single
- Track: narrow gauge
- Bridges, footpath
- Tunnel
- Viaduct
- Freight line, siding or tramway
- Station, (a) principal, (b) closed to passengers
- LC — Level crossing
- Embankment
- Cutting

Rock features

outcrop
650
cliff
600
scree

Public rights of way indicated by these symbols have been derived from Definitive Maps as amended by the latest enactments or instruments held by Ordnance Survey and are shown subject to the limitations imposed by the scale of mapping. Further information may be obtained from the appropriate County or London Borough Council

The representation on this map of any other road, track or path is no evidence of the existence of a right of way

Water features

Canal (dry)

Canal

Lake

Aqueduct

Towpath Lock

Ford

Weir Footbridge Bridge

Normal tidal limit

Marsh or salting

Slopes

Cliff

Flat rock

Sand
Dunes

High water mark

Low water mark

Lighthouse (in use)

Lighthouse (disused)

Mud

Beacon

Shingle

General features

⌄—⌄—⌄	Electricity transmission line (with pylons spaced conventionally)
> - -> - ->	Pipeline (arrow indicates direction of flow)
	Buildings
	Public buildings (selected)
	Bus or coach station
	Coniferous wood
	Non-coniferous wood
	Mixed wood
	Orchard
	Park or ornamental grounds
	Quarry
	Spoil heap, refuse tip or dump
	Radio or TV mast
	Church or chapel with tower
	Church or chapel with spire
+	Church or chapel without tower or spire
○	Chimney or tower
	Glasshouse
+	Graticule intersection at 5' intervals
Ⓗ	Heliport
△	Triangulation pillar
	Windmill with or without sails
	Windpump

Boundaries

+ — + — +	National
-○-○-○-○-	London borough
	National park or forest park
NT	National Trust
—·—·—·—	County, region or islands area
-+-+-+-	District

NT open access

NT limited access

Abbreviations

P	Post office
PH	Public house
MS	Milestone
MP	Milepost
CH	Clubhouse
PC	Public convenience (in rural areas)
TH	Town hall, guildhall or equivalent
CG	Coastguard

Antiquities

VILLA	Roman
Castle	Non-Roman
✕	Battlefield (with date)
☆	Tumulus
+	Position of antiquity which cannot be drawn to scale
ᴟ	Ancient monuments and historic buildings in the care of the Secretaries of State for the Environment, for Scotland and for Wales and that are open to the public

Heights

50	Contours are at 10 metres vertical interval
·144	Heights are to the nearest metre above mean sea level

Heights shown close to a triangulation pillar refer to the station height at ground level and not necessarily to the summit

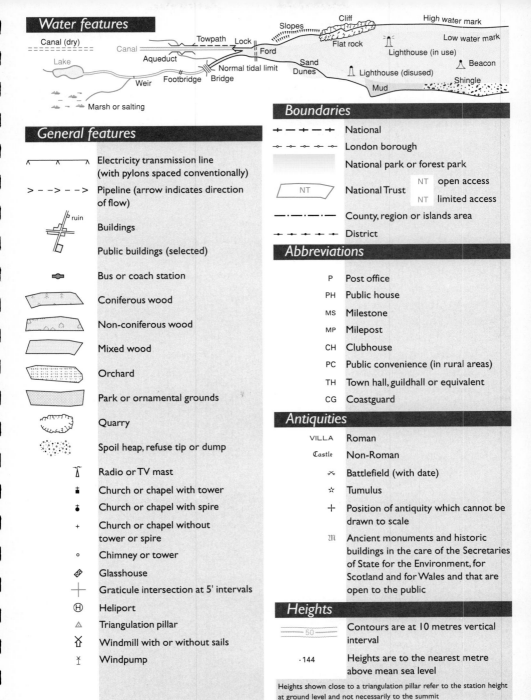

From Richmond over The Stang into Arkengarthdale

Start

Tourist Information Centre, Richmond (near the Turf Hotel, King Street)

P Follow signs off the A6108 Leyburn Road in Richmond

Richmond is the gateway to the Yorkshire Dales from the northeast. The ride heads northwest along the eastern edge of the fells and over the watershed separating the River Swale and the lands drained by the River Tees. After passing through a series of small villages the route turns south and begins to climb through the forestry plantations of The Stang, to the summit of Hope Moor, with wide-ranging views on clear days. The descent takes you down into Arkengarthdale and Reeth – a delightful village. Two further climbs of around 150 m (500 ft) take you up to the masts on Richmond Out Moor with a long, fast descent back to the start.

Distance and grade

50 km (31 miles)
Strenuous

Terrain

Four main climbs: 120 m (400 ft) northwest from Richmond; 365-m (1200-ft) climb from Gayles to the top of Hope Moor; 140 m (470 ft) up from the River Swale, near Reeth, towards Marske and 150-m (500-ft) climb between Marske and Richmond. Lowest point – 130 m

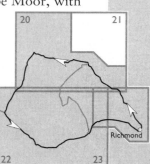

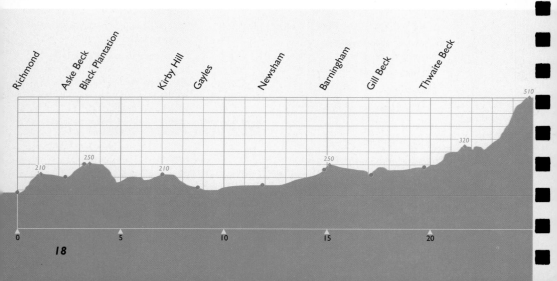

18

(430 ft) in Richmond. Highest point – 520 m (1700 ft) on Hope Moor

Nearest railway

Darlington, 19 km (12 miles) northeast of Richmond

Places of interest

Richmond 1
The Norman castle, with its 30 m (100 ft) high keep, towers dramatically over the River Swale and the cobbled market place. The beautifully restored Theatre Royal survives from the 18th century

The Stang 7
Stunning views of the the Pennines and Teesdale. From the 470-m (1550-ft) cliff edge of Hope Scar, Barnard Castle, Durham Cathedral and even the North Sea are visible on a clear day

◄ *The River Swale at Richmond*

Refreshments

Black Lion PH 🍴, *plenty of choice in* **Richmond**
Shoulder of Mutton PH 🍴🍴, **Kirby Hill**
Bay Horse Inn, **Gayles**
Travellers Rest PH, **Dalton**
Milbank Arms, **Barningham**
Red Lion PH 🍴, Charles Bathurst PH,
Langthwaite
Black Bull PH 🍴, Kings Arms PH 🍴,
plenty of choice in **Reeth**

Hope Moor
Arkengarthdale
Arkle Town
Reeth
Marske
Richmond Out Moor

510

400
290 270 330
320 290 270
180
310
260
130

25   30   35   40   45   50

19

1 With back to the Tourist Information Centre in Richmond (at the roundabout by the Turf Hotel at the end of King Street) L on A6108 'Scotch Corner, Trading Estate'

2 At roundabout SA. At traffic lights L 'Ravensworth 5'

3 Easy to miss – 5 km (3½ miles) from Richmond ignore a left turn signposted 'Marske, Reeth'. Take the next L at offset X-roads (your right of way) 'Kirby Hill ½, Gayles 1¼'

4 Go through Kirby Hill and Gayles. At T-j by Travellers Rest PH in Dalton R 'Newsham 1½' then immediately L

5 At X-roads in Newsham L 'Barningham 1½'. Follow signs for Scargill through Barningham (**Or** for short cut, turn L at X-roads in Newsham then 1st L and follow this for 6 km (10 miles) to Marske, rejoining at instruction 11)

6 At T-j 5 km (3½ miles) after Barningham L 'Reeth 9½'

7 Climb through forestry onto moorland plateau

➡ **page 23**

12 Climb to the masts on Richmond Out Moor then descend to Richmond. At T-j at the end of Hurgill Road, at the bottom of long hill, L 'Market Place, Castle' to return to start

8 *Descend, cross bridge and climb. At T-j L 'Reeth 3½' (**Or** for link to Route 2 turn R 'Tan Hill 7½' to join the other route at instruction 2/3)*

9 *Follow this road past Red Lion PH and Charles Bathurst PH. Climb to 350 m (1150 ft) then descend to Reeth. At T-j with B6270 by the Buck Hotel in Reeth L 'Leyburn 8, Richmond 11'. (**For link** to Route 3*

turn R at T-j 'Gunnerside 6, Kirkby Stephen 23' and join the other route at instruction 7/8)

10 *Through Reeth. 800 m (½ mile) after crossing bridge ignore left turn by stone barn and left turn onto No Through Road. Shortly, on sharp RH bend next L 'Marrick 2½, Marske 4¼, Hurst 4½' (**Or** to avoid next two climbs, by following the river*

valley, do not turn left but follow the B6270 to the A6108, then turn L to return to Richmond)

11 *Steep climb, fast descent.* **Easy to miss** – *At the bottom of steep descent at the start of Marske bear L by triangle of grass with tree 'Whashton 5, Ravensworth 6¼'*

← page 20

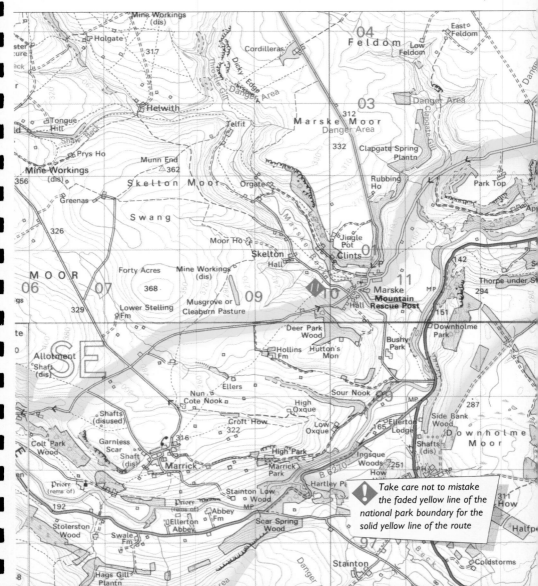

Take care not to mistake the faded yellow line of the national park boundary for the solid yellow line of the route

2 Tan Hill and Swaledale, west of Reeth

Reeth, with its pubs and tea shops around the broad green, is a delightful place to finish a ride. The ride follows Arkengarthdale northwest through the small settlement of Langthwaite and along hillsides. The scenery becomes bleaker as you climb gently over several kilometres to the head of Arkle Beck. It is on bleak moorland that you suddenly come across the Tan Hill Inn – the highest inn in England – then, contrary to all rules of cycling, a long descent follows. The return along Swaledale is as picturesque as any in the Dales with views both along the valley and to the hills to the north and south.

Start

The main square in Reeth, 13 km (8 miles) west of Richmond

P In and around the main square. Please donate to the honesty box

Distance and grade

43 km (27 miles)

Moderate/ strenuous

Terrain

Two steady climbs: 130-m (420-ft) climb along Arkengarthdale; 280 m (930 ft) over 13 km (8 miles) from Langthwaite to Tan Hill Inn. Lowest point – 190 m (630 ft) between Feetham and Healaugh. Highest point – 535 m (1758 ft) at the Tan Hill Inn

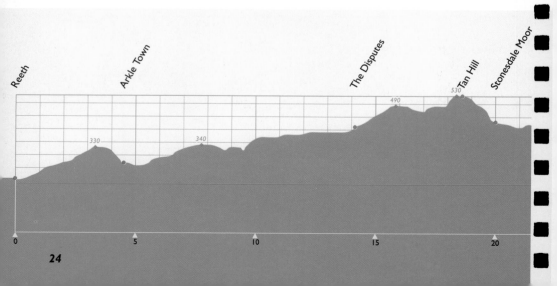

Nearest railway

Garsdale Head, 18 km (11 miles) southwest of Thwaite

Refreshments

Black Bull PH 🍺, Kings Arms 🍺, plenty of choice in **Reeth**
Red Lion PH 🍺, Charles Bathurst PH, **Langthwaite**
Tan Hill Inn 🍺, **Tan Hill**
Farmers Arms 🍺🍺, tea rooms, **Muker**
Kings Head PH, **Gunnerside**
Punch Bowl Inn 🍺, **Feetham**

Places of interest

Reeth 1
During the 19th century this one-time market town became a busy centre for the lead-mining industry of nearby Arkengarthdale. The Swaledale Folk Museum displays artefacts on lead mining and the social life of the dale

Tan Hill 3
A drovers' road across the 535-m (1758-ft) summit of Tan Hill, haunt of grouse and Swaledale sheep and home of the Tan Hill Inn, England's highest inn. Arkengarthdale moor stretches to the east and Stonesdale Moor to the south

Kisdon Gorge 4
The River Swale tumbles through this thickly wooded glen near the granite hamlet of Keld

◄ *Swaledale, near Gunnerside*

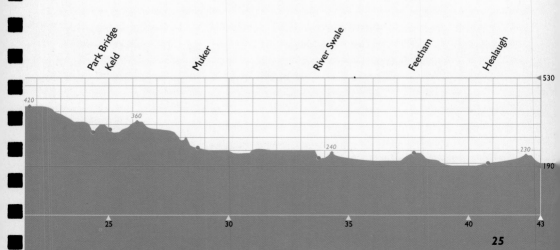

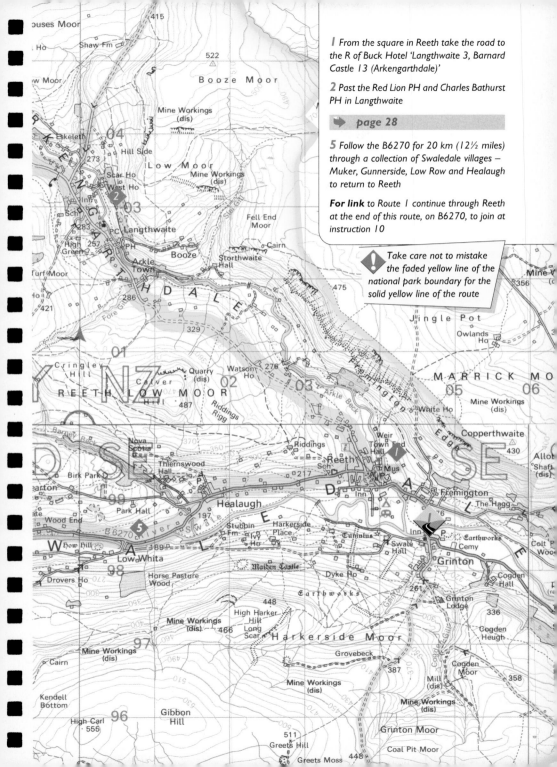

1 *From the square in Reeth take the road to the R of Buck Hotel 'Langthwaite 3, Barnard Castle 13 (Arkengarthdale)'*

2 *Past the Red Lion PH and Charles Bathurst PH in Langthwaite*

➡ **page 28**

5 *Follow the B6270 for 20 km (12½ miles) through a collection of Swaledale villages – Muker, Gunnerside, Low Row and Healaugh to return to Reeth*

For link *to Route 1 continue through Reeth at the end of this route, on B6270, to join at instruction 10*

⚠ *Take care not to mistake the faded yellow line of the national park boundary for the solid yellow line of the route*

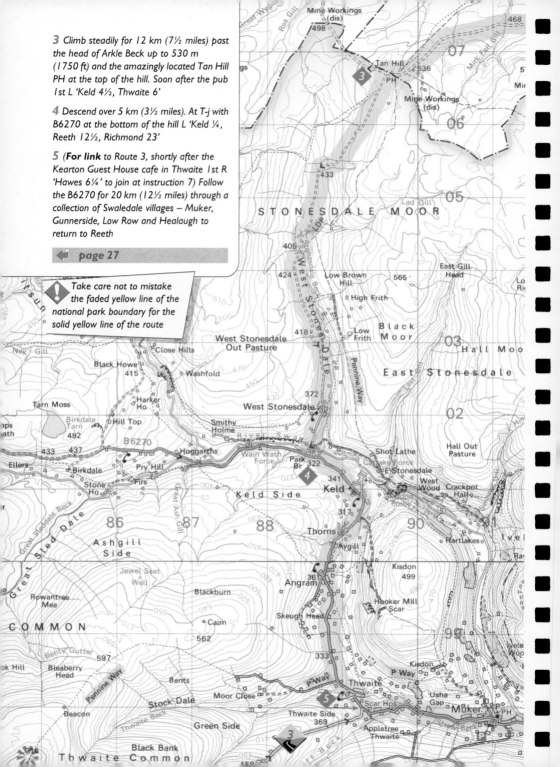

3 Climb steadily for 12 km (7½ miles) past the head of Arkle Beck up to 530 m (1750 ft) and the amazingly located Tan Hill PH at the top of the hill. Soon after the pub 1st L 'Keld 4½, Thwaite 6'

4 Descend over 5 km (3½ miles). At T-j with B6270 at the bottom of the hill L 'Keld ¼, Reeth 12½, Richmond 23'

5 (**For link** to Route 3, shortly after the Kearton Guest House cafe in Thwaite 1st R 'Hawes 6¼' to join at instruction 7) Follow the B6270 for 20 km (12½ miles) through a collection of Swaledale villages – Muker, Gunnerside, Low Row and Healaugh to return to Reeth

page 27

Take care not to mistake the faded yellow line of the national park boundary for the solid yellow line of the route

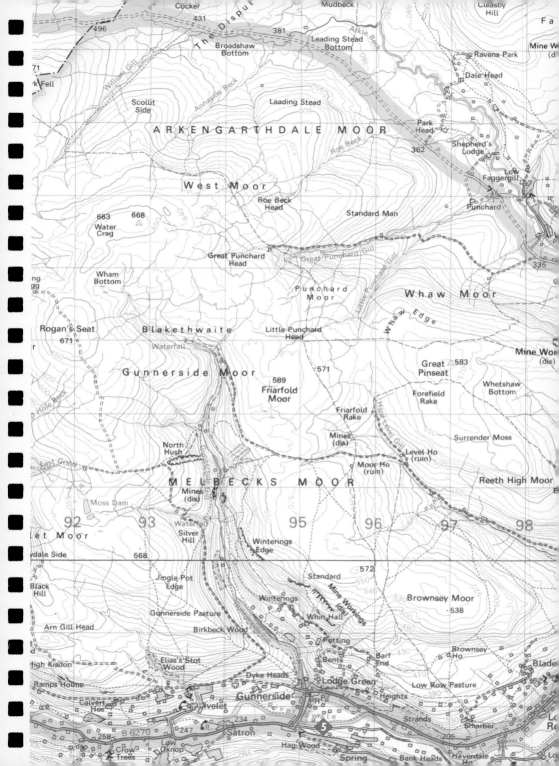

Wensleydale and Swaledale, north of Aysgarth

Start

The car park by the National Park Centre near Aysgarth Falls (signposted off the A684 Northallerton–Sedbergh road)

P As above

If you can resist the challenge of conquering every hill by bike, and are prepared to walk up the short, steep sections, it is quite possible to link two delightful dales which offer gentle cycling along the valleys. This ride is just that – most of it is along Swaledale and Wensleydale but there are perhaps four short sections where the gradient is very steep. The first main climb is up over Redmire and Grinton Moor, dropping down into Grinton and Reeth. West from here the charms of Swaledale are savoured for almost 16 km (10 miles) before the second major climb – over Buttertubs Pass and down into Wensleydale, passing Askrigg where the James Herriot novels were filmed.

Distance and grade

56 km (35 miles) – shorter options are 34 or 42 km (21 or 26 miles)

〰〰〰〰〰 Strenuous

Terrain

Two valleys linked by two steep climbs: 210 m (700 ft) north from Redmire; 270 m (900 ft) southwest from Muker. Lowest point – 150 m (490 ft) at Redmire. Highest point – 520 m (1700 ft) at Butter Tubs pass

▶ Butter Tubs Pass

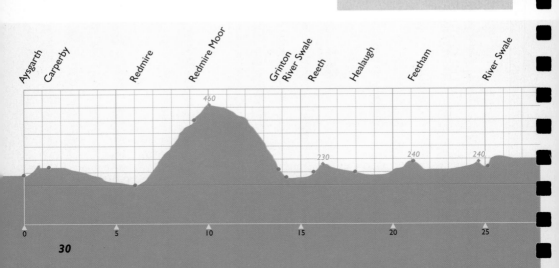

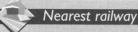

Nearest railway

Garsdale Head, 10 km (6 miles) west of the route at instruction 11

Refreshments

George & Dragon PH 🍴, Palmer Flatt Hotel 🍴, tearooms, **Aysgarth**
Wheatsheaf PH 🍴, **Carperby**
Kings Arms 🍴🍴, Bolton Arms, **Redmire**
Bridge Inn, **Grinton**   Black Bull PH 🍴,
Kings Arms 🍴, plenty of choice in **Reeth**
Punch Bowl Inn 🍴, **Feetham**
Kings Head PH, **Gunnerside**
Farmers Arms 🍴🍴, tea rooms, **Muker**
Crown Inn, Kings Arms 🍴🍴, tea shops, **Askrigg**

Places of interest

Aysgarth 1
The River Ure cascades over three spectacular falls in the tree-lined gorge. The former cotton mill is now a carriage museum

Castle Bolton 3
Mary, Queen of Scots was locked up for six months in this 14th-century castle, overshadowing stone cottages that fringe the village green. The nearby 14th-century church houses local exhibitions

Butter Tubs Pass 10/11
Named after the deep limestone shafts that pock the countryside a short distance from the road. It is thought that these may have been dug by farmers and used to cool and harden butter that had got too warm on the way to market

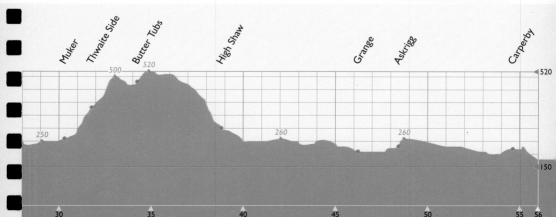

Take care not to mistake the faded yellow line of the national park boundary for the solid yellow line of the route

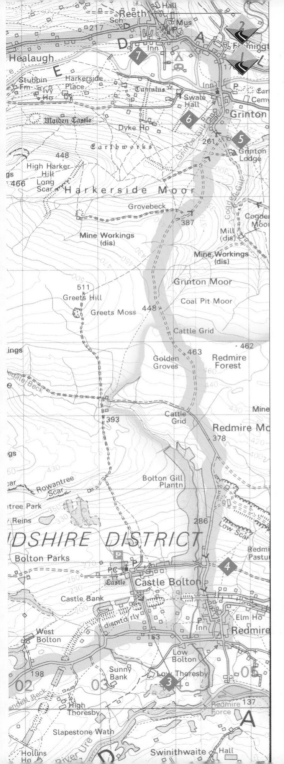

1 Out of the Aysgarth Falls/National Park Centre car park and turn L under the bridge

2 At T-j in Carperby by triangle of grass with tree R 'Castle Bolton 3, Redmire 3, Leyburn 8'

3 For Castle Bolton: 4 km (2½ miles) after Carperby 1st L 'Castle Bolton', then at T-j 1 km after the castle L uphill 'Grinton 4, Reeth 5'. For Redmire: cross bridge over stream then 1st L 'Post Office and Stores, Kings Arms'. At T-j by triangle of grass L past Bolton Arms

4 Routes join and climb hill to high point at 460 m (1500 ft)

5 Fast descent. At T-j L 'Reeth 1½'

6 At T-j with B6270 by the Bridge Inn in Grinton bear L 'Reeth ¾' (**For link** to Route 1, cross bridge then 1st R at the start of Fremington 'Marrick, Marske, Hurst' and join the other route at instruction 10)

7 Follow the B6270 into and through Reeth, following signs for Gunnerside and Kirkby Stephen. (**For link** to Route 2 turn R at the Buck Hotel in Reeth 'Langthwaite, Barnard Castle' and join the other route at instruction 1)

8 Follow the B6270 along Wensleydale through Healaugh, Gunnerside and Muker. (For short cut 1st L after Healaugh 'Askrigg 6½' then shortly at T-j R 'Askrigg 6')

➡ *page 34*

13 After a further 6 km (4 miles) shortly after sign for Caperby, at start of village, R 'Aysgarth Falls, National Park Centre' for 2 km (1¼ miles) to return to start

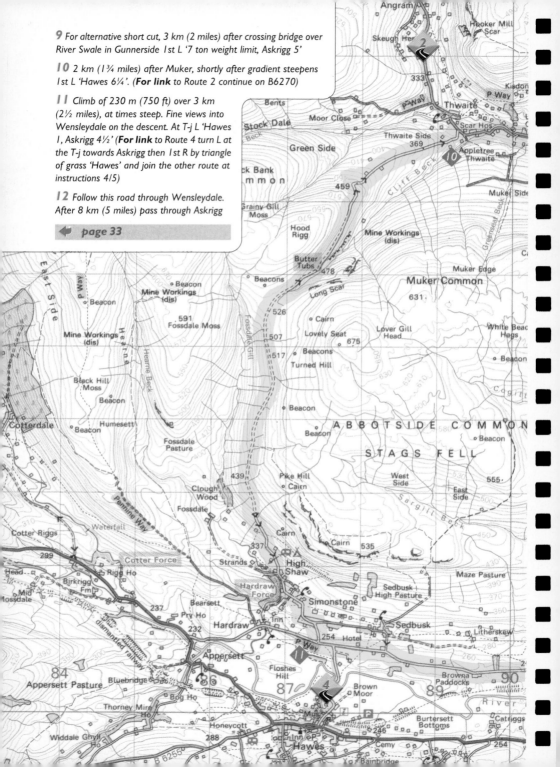

9 *For alternative short cut, 3 km (2 miles) after crossing bridge over River Swale in Gunnerside 1st L '7 ton weight limit, Askrigg 5'*

10 *2 km (1¾ miles) after Muker, shortly after gradient steepens 1st L 'Hawes 6¼'. (**For link** to Route 2 continue on B6270)*

11 *Climb of 230 m (750 ft) over 3 km (2½ miles), at times steep. Fine views into Wensleydale on the descent. At T-j L 'Hawes 1, Askrigg 4½' (**For link** to Route 4 turn L at the T-j towards Askrigg then 1st R by triangle of grass 'Hawes' and join the other route at instructions 4/5)*

12 *Follow this road through Wensleydale. After 8 km (5 miles) pass through Askrigg*

◀ *page 33*

From Aysgarth to Hubberholme

The direction chosen for this ride is westwards along the spectacular beauty of Wensleydale to the popular tourist destination of Hawes. The climb up over Fleet Moss is fairly demanding, particularly one horribly steep section near the top. The descent lasts several kilometres as it follows Oughtershaw Beck, then the River Wharfe, down to Hubberholme and a very fine pub. The return to Aysgarth involves the second major climb of the day, although not nearly as long or as tough as the first climb up from Hawes. Magnificent views down Bishopdale and into Wensleydale open up from the summit at the top of Kidsones Scar. Two final short, sharp climbs either side of the main road in Aysgarth bring you back to the start.

Start

The car park by the National Park Centre near Aysgarth Falls (signposted off the A684 Northallerton–Sedbergh road)

P As above

Distance and grade

48 km (30 miles)

Strenuous

Terrain

Two climbs: 350 m (1150 ft) from Hawes to Bardale Head; 185 m (610 ft) from

Refreshments

George & Dragon PH ✸, Palmer Flatt Hotel ✸, tearooms, **Aysgarth**
Crown Inn, Kings Arms ✸✸, tea shops, **Askrigg**
Crown PH ✸, plenty of choice in **Hawes**
George Inn ✸✸, **Hubberholme**
White Lion PH ✸✸, **Cray**
George PH ✸, Street Head Inn, **Thoralby**

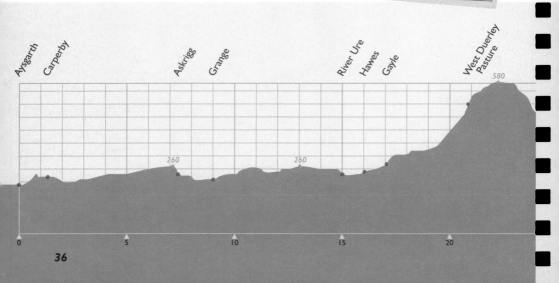

Hubberholme to
Kidstones Scar. Lowest
point – 150 m (500 ft)
at West Burton.
Highest point – 590 m
(1950 ft) at the pass
between Wensleydale
and Langstrothdale

Nearest railway

Garsdale Head, 10 km
(6 miles) west of
Hawes

► *Wensleydale near Hawes*

Places of interest

Bainbridge *3/4 (just off the route)*
A hunting horn is blown on the village green
on dark evenings, a tradition from when
forest workers had to be guided home. The
track by the River Bain follows the old
Roman road and there are remains of a
Roman fort nearby

Hawes 5
Among the old ways of life illustrated in the
Upper Dales Folk Museum are local crafts
and equipment used for cheese and butter
making, sheep shearing and lead mining

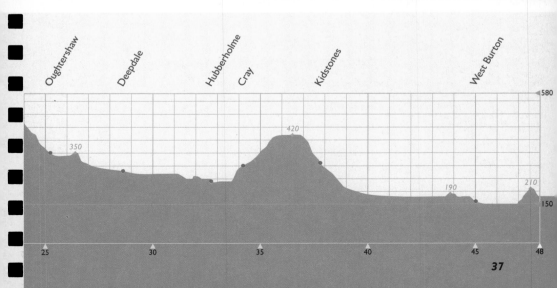

1 Out of the Aysgarth Falls/ National Park Centre car park and turn L under the bridge

2 At T-j in Carperby by triangle of grass with tree L 'Askrigg 4¼, Hawes 9¾' (**See also** Route 3 for longer loop, turning R here 'Castle Bolton 3, Redmire 3, Leyburn 8' and rejoining route at instruction 4)

3 Keep eye out for attractive and unusual Nappa Hall to the left. Through Askrigg, along through Wensleydale

4 **Easy to miss** – 9 km (5½ miles) after Askrigg, shortly after the Stone House Country Hotel and a right turn to Sedbusk, next L by a triangle of grass 'Hawes'

5 At X-roads with A684 in Hawes SA 'Sedbergh 16, Ingleton 16'

6 Towards the end of Hawes 1st proper L by primary school 'Gayle ½, Kettlewell 15' (**Or** follow B6255 to Newby Head Moss for link to Route 8 at instruction 8)

➡ **page 41**

12 Descend. 2 km (1½ miles) after the Street Head Inn in Thoralby and shortly after passing a bridge on your right 'Unsuitable for motors' next L 'Aysgarth 1½, Hawes 10½'

13 At T-j with A684 L uphill then 1st R by the Palmer Flatt Hotel 'Aysgarth Falls ¼, Carperby 1' to return to the start

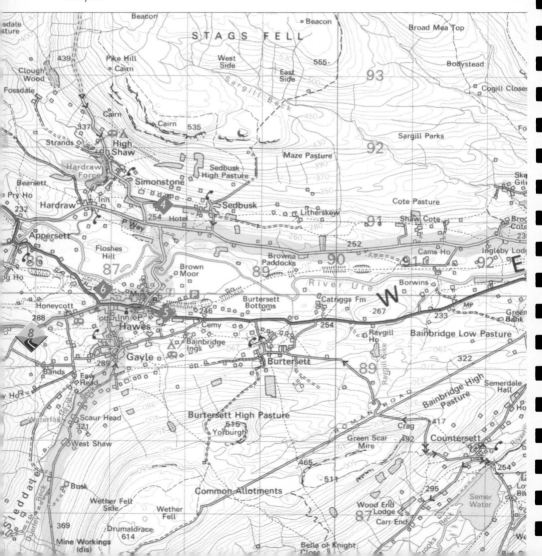

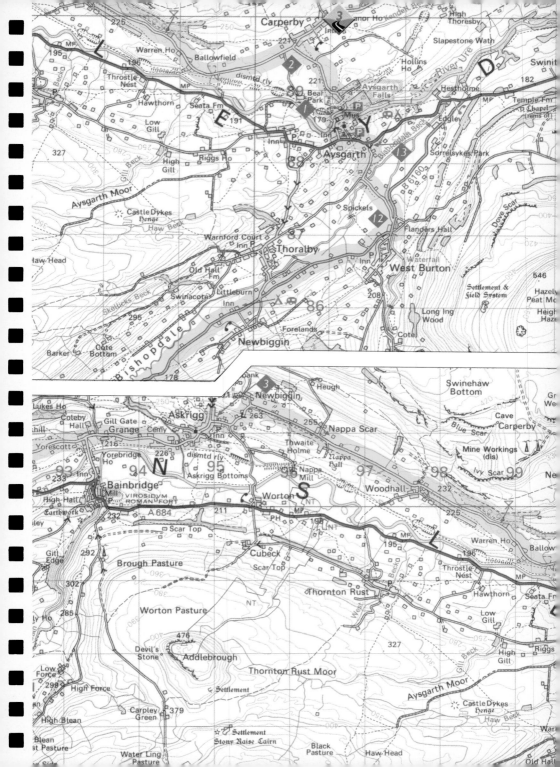

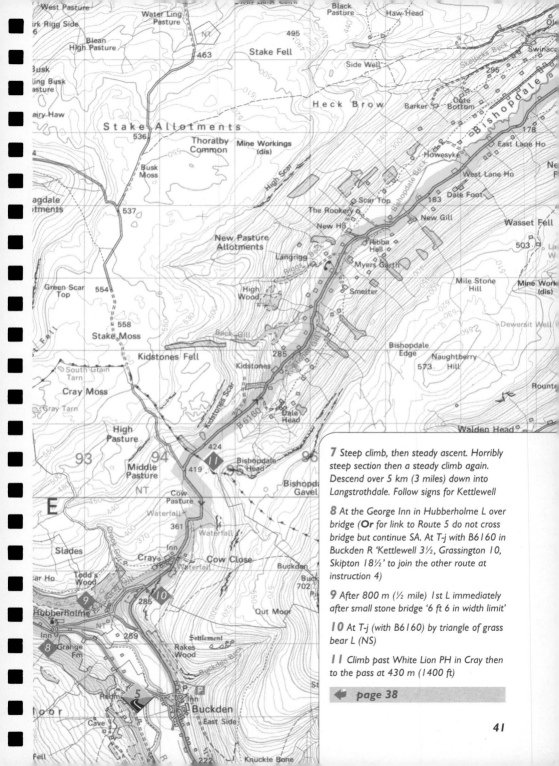

7 Steep climb, then steady ascent. Horribly steep section then a steady climb again. Descend over 5 km (3 miles) down into Langstrothdale. Follow signs for Kettlewell

8 At the George Inn in Hubberholme L over bridge (**Or** for link to Route 5 do not cross bridge but continue SA. At T-j with B6160 in Buckden R 'Kettlewell 3½, Grassington 10, Skipton 18½' to join the other route at instruction 4)

9 After 800 m (½ mile) 1st L immediately after small stone bridge '6 ft 6 in width limit'

10 At T-j (with B6160) by triangle of grass bear L (NS)

11 Climb past White Lion PH in Cray then to the pass at 430 m (1400 ft)

← page 38

5 *From Aysgarth to Kettlewell*

The last of the five rides, based on Swaledale and Wensleydale, that can all be linked together to form one long loop – suitable for a tour over several days. The very steep climb by Aysgarth waterfalls starts the day but is soon followed by a gentle ride along Bishopdale which steepens after about 8 km (5 miles). There are wide-ranging views from

◄ *Kettlewell in Wharfedale*

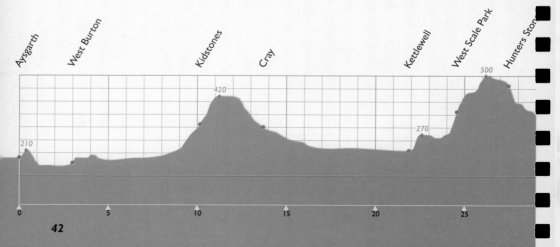

Aysgarth · West Burton · Kidstones · Cray · Kettlewell · West Scale Park · Hunters Ston

500
420
270
210

0   5   10   15   20   25

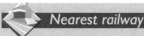
Gargrave, 24 km (15 miles) south of Kettlewell

Refreshments

George & Dragon PH 🍴, Palmer Flatt Hotel 🍴, tearooms **Aysgarth**
George PH 🍴, Street Head Inn, **Thoralby**
White Lion Inn 🍴🍴, **Cray**
Buck Inn Hotel 🍴🍴, tea rooms, **Buckden**
Fox & Hounds PH 🍴🍴, **Starbotton**
Kings Head PH 🍴, Bluebell Hotel 🍴, Racehorses Hotel 🍴, **Kettlewell**
Thwaites Inn, **Horsehouse**
Foresters Arms 🍴🍴, **Carlton**
Three Horseshoes PH, **Wensley**
Kings Arms 🍴🍴, Bolton Arms, **Redmire**
Wheatsheaf PH 🍴, **Carperby**

the top of the pass before a fast descent into Wharfedale. There is a string of pubs at regular intervals to prepare you for one of the toughest climbs in the book which occurs about 3 km (2 miles) after Kettlewell at a gradient of 1:4. You then follow the River Cover to the northeast – the very edge of the Dales – before heading west and back to Aysgarth.

Places of interest

Kettlewell 6
Its heyday was in the 17th–19th century as a market town and lead mining centre. At the western end of the village both the Bluebell Hotel (built in 1680) and the nearby Racehorses Hotel have cobbled forecourts and whitewashed walls, contrasting with the natural stone used elsewhere in the village. Across the beck, near the old stone bridge, stands a shop that used to house the blacksmith's forge

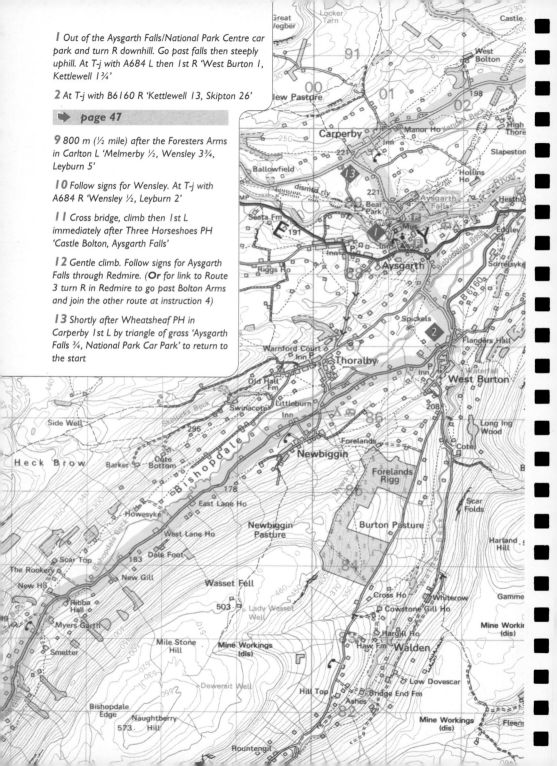

1 Out of the Aysgarth Falls/National Park Centre car park and turn R downhill. Go past falls then steeply uphill. At T-j with A684 L then 1st R 'West Burton 1, Kettlewell 1¾'

2 At T-j with B6160 R 'Kettlewell 13, Skipton 26'

➡ **page 47**

9 800 m (½ mile) after the Foresters Arms in Carlton L 'Melmerby ½, Wensley 3¾, Leyburn 5'

10 Follow signs for Wensley. At T-j with A684 R 'Wensley ½, Leyburn 2'

11 Cross bridge, climb then 1st L immediately after Three Horseshoes PH 'Castle Bolton, Aysgarth Falls'

12 Gentle climb. Follow signs for Aysgarth Falls through Redmire. (**Or** for link to Route 3 turn R in Redmire to go past Bolton Arms and join the other route at instruction 4)

13 Shortly after Wheatsheaf PH in Carperby 1st L by triangle of grass 'Aysgarth Falls ¾, National Park Car Park' to return to the start

Take care not to mistake
the faded yellow line of the
national park boundary for the
solid yellow line of the route

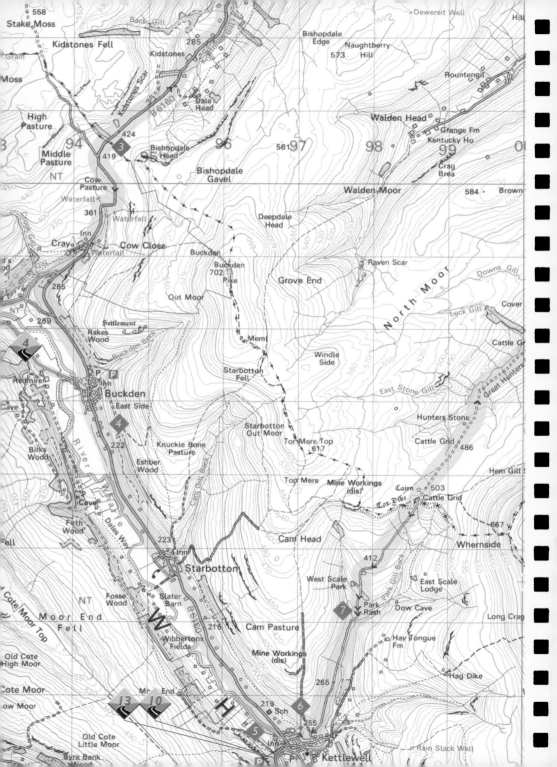

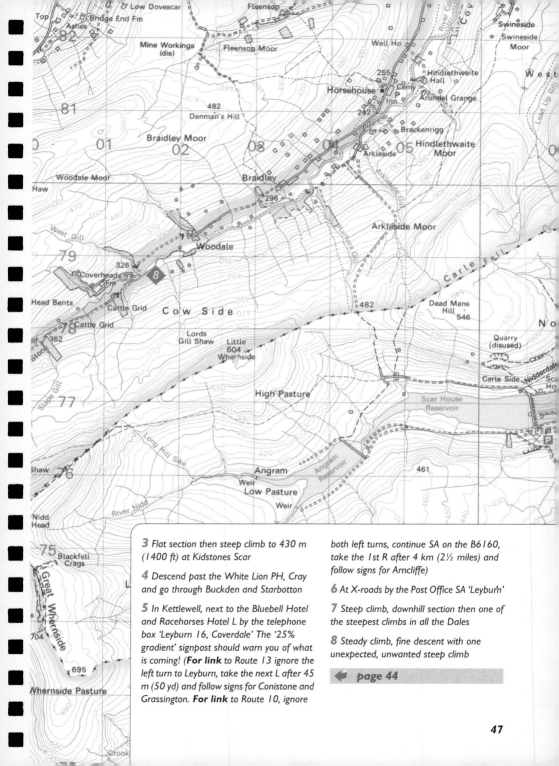

3 Flat section then steep climb to 430 m (1400 ft) at Kidstones Scar

4 Descend past the White Lion PH, Cray and go through Buckden and Starbotton

5 In Kettlewell, next to the Bluebell Hotel and Racehorses Hotel L by the telephone box 'Leyburn 16, Coverdale' The '25% gradient' signpost should warn you of what is coming! (**For link** to Route 13 ignore the left turn to Leyburn, take the next L after 45 m (50 yd) and follow signs for Conistone and Grassington. **For link** to Route 10, ignore

both left turns, continue SA on the B6160, take the 1st R after 4 km (2½ miles) and follow signs for Arncliffe)

6 At X-roads by the Post Office SA 'Leyburn'

7 Steep climb, downhill section then one of the steepest climbs in all the Dales

8 Steady climb, fine descent with one unexpected, unwanted steep climb

◀ **page 44**

6 From Pateley Bridge to Masham, returning along Nidderdale

Start

Pateley Bridge Hotel, 24 km (15 miles) northwest of Harrogate on the B6265

P Follow signs

Distance and grade

45 km (28 miles)

Strenuous

Terrain

Two main climbs: 210 m (680 ft) from Pateley Bridge up to Brownstay Ridge (very steep section at the start); 290 m (950 ft) from River Burn, near Healey, southwest onto High Ash Head Moor. Lowest point – 80 m (260 ft) at the River Ure, south of Masham. Highest point – 430 m (1400 ft) at High Ash Head Moor

*T*he climb from Pateley Bridge is so steep and so soon after the start that you are well advised to walk up it and admire the views as they open up behind you. You are soon on the top of heather-clad moorland with the views now to the northeast towards the Hambleton Hills. Masham is a large attractive village at the northern end of the ride. The villages and settlements thin out as the ride heads southwest and climbs to the top of High Ash Head Moor – views to the southwest are spectacular. The 10 km (6½ miles) along Nidderdale are lovely cycling.

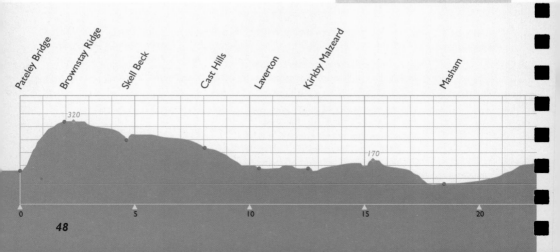

Knaresborough, 24 km (15 miles) southeast of Pateley Bridge

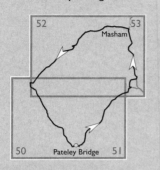

▶ The Saxon cross at St Mary's, Masham

Pateley Bridge 1
Small town with a main street of stone cottages. The old workhouse (1863) is now the Nidderdale Museum, featuring domestic, farming and industrial bygones. West of the town are the fascinating Stump Cross Caverns

Masham 9
The huge square, dominated by a Market Cross, indicates Masham's former importance as a market town. In the churchyard of St Mary's are important remains of a Saxon cross

How Stean Gorge 11
A dramatic ravine in the Carboniferous limestone, 24 m (80 ft) deep in places. Viewpoints overlook the cascades

Crown PH, Royal Oak PH, tea shops in **Pateley Bridge**
Drovers Inn 🍴, south of **Laverton**
Henry Jenkins Inn, Quens Head PH, **Kirkby Malzeard**
Crown PH, **Grewelthorpe**
Kings Head PH 🍴🍴, White Bear PH 🍴🍴, **Masham**
Kings Head PH, Black Swan Inn, **Fearby**
Crown Inn, How Steam Gorge Cafe, **Lofthouse**
Yorke Arms 🍴🍴, **Ramsgill**
Sportsmans Arms 🍴🍴, **Wath**

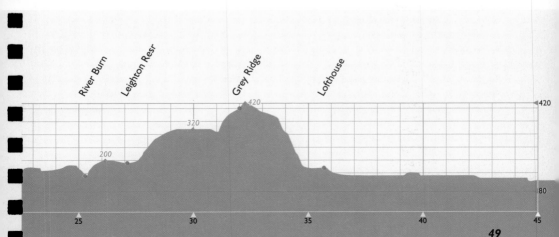

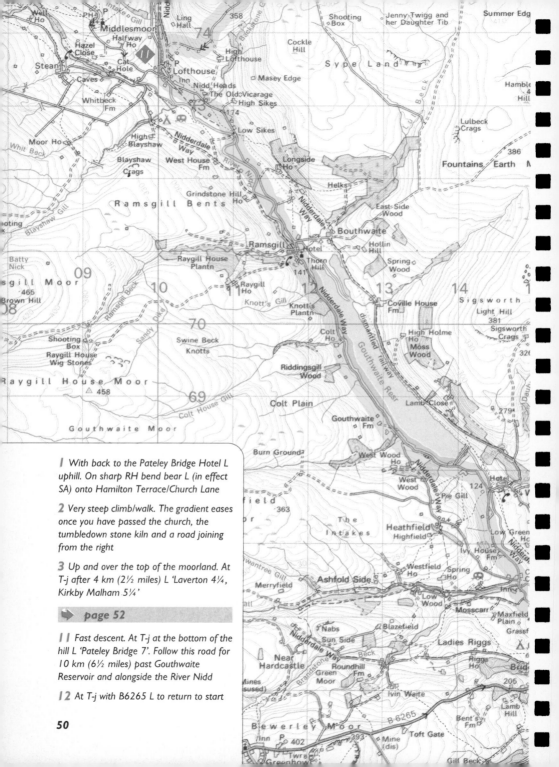

1 With back to the Pateley Bridge Hotel L uphill. On sharp RH bend bear L (in effect SA) onto Hamilton Terrace/Church Lane

2 Very steep climb/walk. The gradient eases once you have passed the church, the tumbledown stone kiln and a road joining from the right

3 Up and over the top of the moorland. At T-j after 4 km (2½ miles) L 'Laverton 4¼, Kirkby Malham 5¼'

➡ *page 52*

11 Fast descent. At T-j at the bottom of the hill L 'Pateley Bridge 7'. Follow this road for 10 km (6½ miles) past Gouthwaite Reservoir and alongside the River Nidd

12 At T-j with B6265 L to return to start

4 After 4 km (2½ miles) ignore 1st left to Laverton, immediately after Drovers Inn. Next L 'Laverton ½, Kirkby Malzeard 1½'

5 At T-j in Laverton L 'Kirkby Malham 5¾' (**Or** for link to Route 7 turn R 'Galphay, Grantley' then at T-j R 'Galphay, Ripon' to join the other route at instruction 15)

6 At the end of Kirkby Malzeard bear L by the X-roads sign past Queens Head PH then at T-j after 46 m (50 yd) L 'Grewelthorpe 1½, Masham 4¾'

7 At T-j by Give Way sign R

8 After 2 km (1¼ miles) 1st R by triangle of grass 'Grewelthorpe, Masham 3' then shortly at T-j by the Crown PH L 'Masham 3¼'

9 Follow road into Masham. Shortly after square to the right and Bayhorse Inn to the left bear L immediately after Post Office

'Middleham 8¾, Leyburn 10¾'. At T-j with A6048 L 'Middleham' then 2nd L 'Fearby 1½, Healey 2½, Leighton 4'

10 Follow this road through Fearby and Healey and descend to cross the River Burn. Climb 290 m (950 ft) over 5 km (3½ miles) with three steep sections

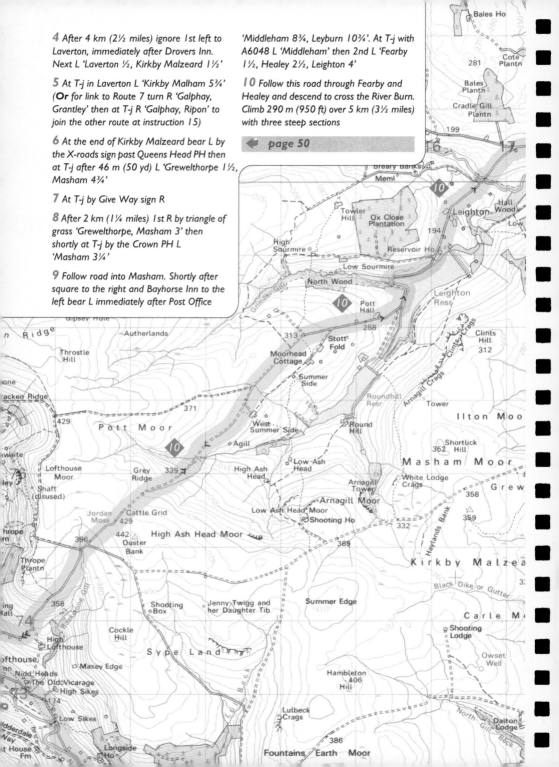

← **page 50**

An easy ride from Ripon to Bedale

Ripon is famous for its cathedral which is well worth a visit. However, one of the main attractions of this ride is the lack of hills – it is the only easy ride in the book. There is a short, unavoidable section on the busy A61 at the start of the ride before heading north on quiet lanes through rich, agricultural country – quite different from the Dales scenery to the west. South from Bedale you have the opportunity to link with Route 6 at the attractive village of Masham. Gently rolling countryside brings you back to Ripon, through the stone-built villages of Grewelthorpe, Kirby Malzeard and Galphay.

Start

Market Square, Ripon
P Follow signs

Distance and grade

51 km (32 miles) – short route 40 km (25 miles)
✏ Easy

Terrain

Two climbs: 90 m (300 ft) southwest from Bedale. 80 m (270 ft) south from Masham. Lowest point – 25 m (80 ft) at River Ure in Ripon. Highest point – 160 m (520 ft) between Masham and Grewelthorpe

Refreshments

Water Rat PH 🍺, *Blackamoor PH* 🍺, *Golden Lion PH* 🍺, **Ripon**   George Inn, **Wath**   Black Horse Inn, **Kirklington** Fox & Hounds PH 🍺🍺, **Carthorpe** Castle Arms 🍺, **Snape**   Thorp Perrow Arboretum Tea Room, Olde Black Swan PH 🍺, **Bedale** Buck Inn 🍺, **Thornton Watlass** Kings Head PH 🍺🍺, White Bear PH 🍺🍺, **Masham** Crown PH, **Grewelthorpe**

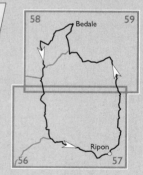

Nearest railway

Thirsk, 11 km (7 miles)
east of the route at
Kirklington

Places of interest

Thorp Perrow Arboretum 7/8
24 ha (60 acres) of landscaped grounds
contain 1000 species of trees and shrubs.
Nearby is Snape Castle – home of Henry
VIII's sixth and last wife, Catherine Parr

Studley Royal and Fountains Abbey 16
Studley Royal estate includes a deer park,
St Mary's church, built by William Burgess
in 1871–1878 and a spectacular early
18th-century garden by John Aislabie. The
extensive ruins of Fountains Abbey, one of
the first monastic foundations to be
dissolved by Henry VIII and the most
complete Cistercian abbey in Britain, form
the centrepiece of the gardens

▼ Fountains Abbey

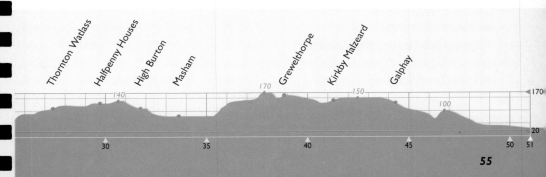

Thornton Watlass · Halfpenny Houses · High Burton · Masham · Grewelthorpe · Kirkby Malzeard · Galphay

170 · 150 · 140 · 100 · 170 · 20

30 · 35 · 40 · 45 · 50 · 51

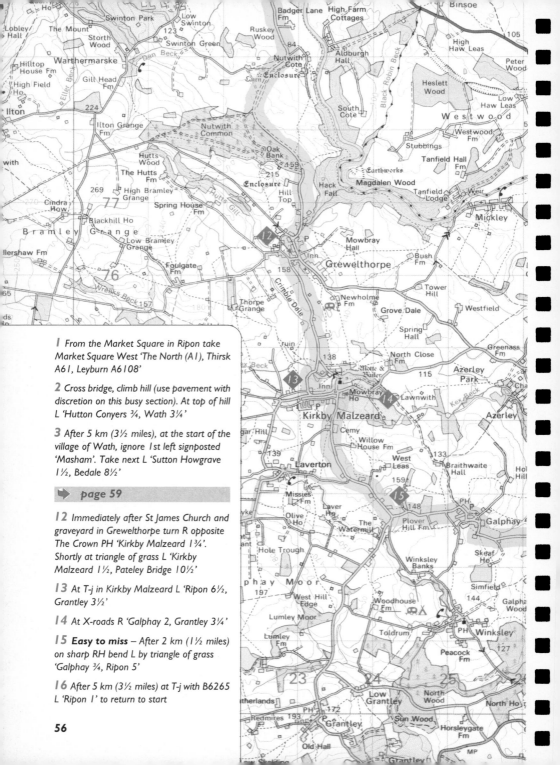

1 From the Market Square in Ripon take Market Square West 'The North (A1), Thirsk A61, Leyburn A6108'

2 Cross bridge, climb hill (use pavement with discretion on this busy section). At top of hill L 'Hutton Conyers ¾, Wath 3¼'

3 After 5 km (3½ miles), at the start of the village of Wath, ignore 1st left signposted 'Masham'. Take next L 'Sutton Howgrave 1½, Bedale 8½'

➡ **page 59**

12 Immediately after St James Church and graveyard in Grewelthorpe turn R opposite The Crown PH 'Kirkby Malzeard 1¾'. Shortly at triangle of grass L 'Kirkby Malzeard 1½, Pateley Bridge 10½'

13 At T-j in Kirkby Malzeard L 'Ripon 6½, Grantley 3½'

14 At X-roads R 'Galphay 2, Grantley 3¼'

15 *Easy to miss* – After 2 km (1½ miles) on sharp RH bend L by triangle of grass 'Galphay ¾, Ripon 5'

16 After 5 km (3½ miles) at T-j with B6265 L 'Ripon 1' to return to start

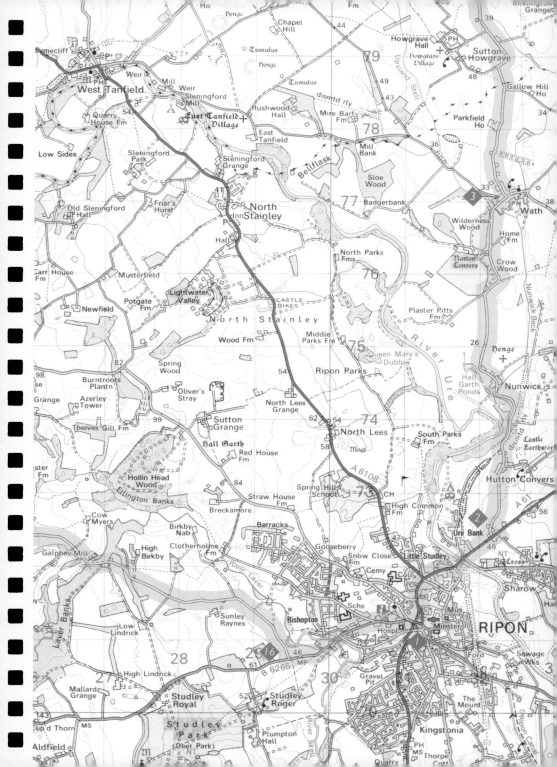

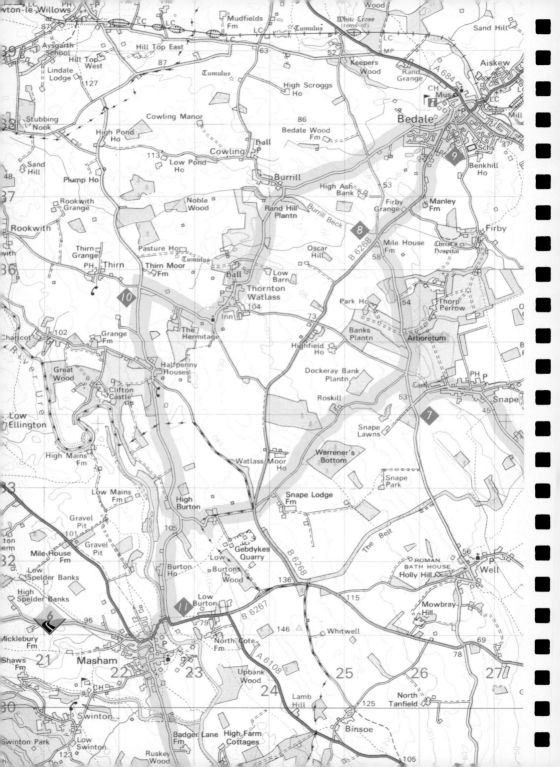

4 At offset X-roads with B6267 SA 'Kirklington ½, Bedale 6¾'

5 At T-j in Kirklington bear L 'Carthorpe 2, Bedale 6'

6 At X-roads (your right of way) in Carthorpe L 'Snape 3, Tanfield 4¼'

7 Through Snape. At T-j R 'Thornton Watlass 2¼, Bedale 2¾' (For short cut, turn R towards Bedale then 1st L 'Masham'. At X-roads with B6268 diagonally L 'High Burton 2'. At T-j at the bottom of the hill L 'Masham' to rejoin route at instruction 11)

8 At T-j (with B6268) R 'Bedale 1½'

9 After visiting Bedale retrace route along Sussex Street 'Masham B6268'. Start climbing. On LH bend bear R onto Burrill Road 'Thornton Watlass 2½, Middleham 10'

10 Through Thornton Watlass and follow road round to the R by the church, ignoring the left turn to Masham. At X-roads L 'Masham 4½'

11 After 4 km (2½ miles) at T-j with A6108 R 'Masham, Middleham, Leyburn' then 1st L after bridge 'Masham, Grewelthorpe' (**Or** SA for link to Route 6 to join the other route at the last part of instruction 9)

◀ page 56

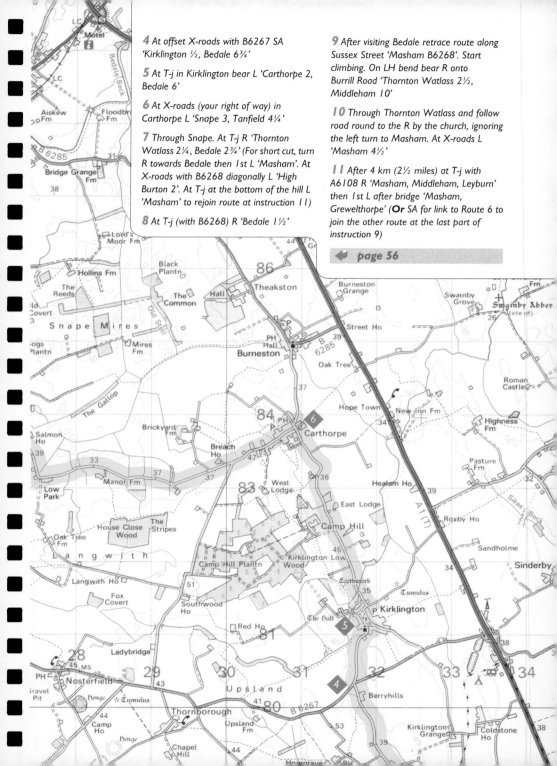

A circuit around Whernside

8

Ingleton is a good base from which to explore the Three Peaks of Whernside, Ingleborough, and Pen-y-Ghent – some of the highest peaks in Yorkshire. The limestone scenery hides a vast network of underground caves and passages, indicated above ground by rivers that dry up, such as Kingsdale Beck, running alongside the delightful, gated road beneath the rock formations of Keld Head Scar. The climb steepens after Kingsdale Head rising to over 460 m (1500 ft) at White Shaw Moss. From Dent there is a gentle start to the climb alongside another disappearing river (the Dee) and passes beneath the first of the extraordinary viaducts. A narrow lane just beyond Chapel-le-Dale passes beneath the limestone cliffs of Twistleton Scar back to Ingleton.

Start

Tourist Information Centre in the main car park, Ingleton (off the A65 between Kirkby Lonsdale and Settle)

P Follow signs for 'Main car park'

Distance and grade

45 km (28 miles)
Moderate/ strenuous

Terrain

Three climbs: 180 m (600 ft) from Ingleton to just north of Thornton in Lonsdale; 170 m (560 ft) from Kingsdale to White Shaw Moss; 290 m (960 ft) from Dent to the B6255 – steep near the head of Dentdale. Lowest point – 115 m (370 ft) in Ingleton. Highest point – 480 m (1570 ft) at White Shaw Moss

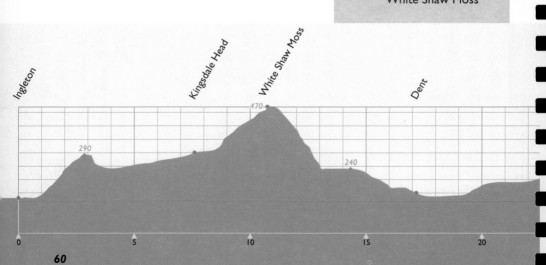

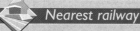
Ribblehead Station is
on the route

Places of interest

Ingleton *1*
Ingleton Glens boast spectacular waterfalls
and fine woodland scenery. White Scar
Cave under
Ingleborough Hill
has stalactites and
two waterfalls

Refreshments

Craven Heifer PH 🍴, plenty of choice in **Ingleton**
Marton Arms 🍴, **Thornton in Lonsdale**
George & Dragon PH, Sun Inn 🍴🍴, tea shops in **Dent**
Sportsmans Inn 🍴, **Cowgill**
Station Inn, **Ribblehead**
New Inn 🍴, **Chapel-le-Dale**

Dent *6*
Picturesque cobbled
village overlooking the
River Dee in lovely
Dentdale. It is
famous for its
hand-knitted
woollens, still
produced locally.

Ribble Head *8/9*
The man-made
spectacle of the
24 arches of the
Settle-Carlisle
railway viaduct
vies with the
natural wonders
of Yorkshire's
Three Peaks

◄ *Dent Head Viaduct*

Take care not to mistake the faded yellow line of the national park boundary for the solid yellow line of the route

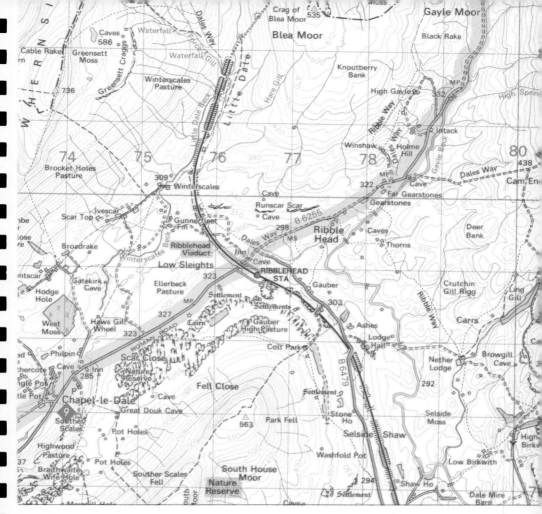

1 From the Tourist Information Centre/main car park follow signs for 'Village Centre'. At T-j with the railway viaduct ahead R then bear L downhill 'Thornton in Lonsdale ¾'. At T-j L downhill over bridge 'Waterfalls'

2 Cross two bridges. 800 m (½ mile) after going under viaduct, on LH bend, bear R 'Thornton in Lonsdale ¼, Dent 10'

3 Follow road round to the R over bridge then soon after the Marton Arms Hotel and church 1st R 'Dent 9½'

4 Steady climb, short descent, long flattish section. Steep climb and fast descent

➡ **page 64**

9 After 5 km (3½ miles) pass beneath the Ribblehead railway viaduct then after futher 3 km (2 miles) go past the New Inn in Chapel-le-Dale. **Easy to miss** – on fast descent 800 m (½ mile) after the pub 1st R 'Chapel-le-Dale church, Single Track Road'

10 Gentle descent then steep hill down into Ingleton

11 At T-j at the end of Mill Lane L then at the start of one way system fork R uphill 'Hawes (B6255) Settle, Skipton (A65)'. At T-j at the top of the hill R then 1st L after going beneath bridge to return to car park (**For link** to Route 9, join at instruction 7)

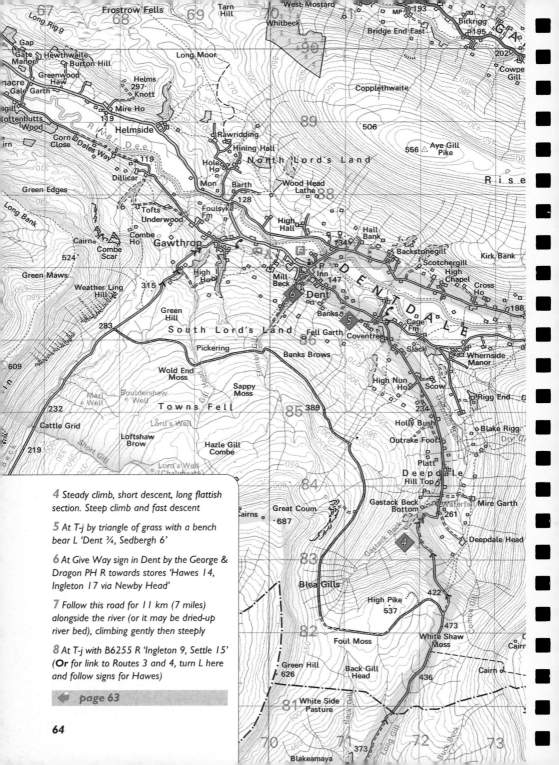

4 Steady climb, short descent, long flattish section. Steep climb and fast descent

5 At T-j by triangle of grass with a bench bear L 'Dent ¾, Sedbergh 6'

6 At Give Way sign in Dent by the George & Dragon PH R towards stores 'Hawes 14, Ingleton 17 via Newby Head'

7 Follow this road for 11 km (7 miles) alongside the river (or it may be dried-up river bed), climbing gently then steeply

8 At T-j with B6255 R 'Ingleton 9, Settle 15' (Or for link to Routes 3 and 4, turn L here and follow signs for Hawes)

◀ page 63

West from Settle to Ingleton and Wray

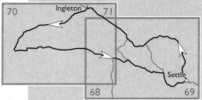

Start

The Royal Oak Hotel in the main square, Settle

P Follow signs

The first of three rides from Settle, a bustling market town. The 'cigar' shape of this route means that all sorts of short cuts are possible and as long as you aim to cross the busy A65 at right angles, all the lanes in the valley formed by the River

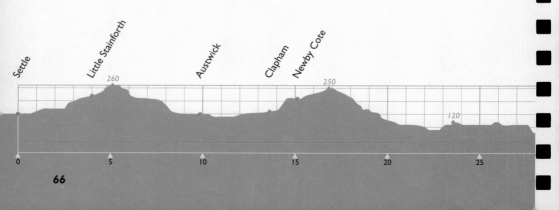

Distance and grade

56 km (35 miles)

Moderate

Terrain

Three climbs: 130 m (430 ft) from Settle to just beyond Little Stainforth; 115 m (380 ft) from the A65 near Austwick towards Ingleton; 130 m (420 ft) from Wray to Keasden. Lowest point – 50 m (155 ft) at the River Hindburn in Wray. Highest point – 260 m (860 ft) just north of Little Stainforth

Nearest railway

Settle

Refreshments

Royal Oak PH ●●, Golden Lion PH ●, **Settle**
Game Cock PH ●●, **Austwick**
New Inn ●, Tea shop, **Clapham**
Craven Heifer ●, plenty of choice in **Ingleton**
Bridge Inn, **Tatham**
George & Dragon PH, **Wray**

◀ Stainforth Force and packhorse bridge

Wenning are appropriate for devising relatively easy cycle rides. Beyond Clapham the ride passes beneath the vast bulk of Ingleborough before dropping down into Ingleton. West from here the ride passes briefly into Lancashire at Wennington and Wray, dropping down to the crossing of the River Hindburn. Quiet lanes then lead east and signs for Settle are soon picked up.

Places of interest

Settle 1
Limestone cliffs overlook this bustling market town with a handsome square, a multitude of small courts and alleyways contained by 18th- and 19th-century houses. The Museum of North Craven life is in Chapel Street

Stainforth 1/2 (just off the route)
A charming waterfall tumbles through a ravine just below the village's 17th-century packhorse bridge over the River Ribble

Clapham 5
Four stone bridges cross the mountain stream of Clapham Beck. Nearby are the exotic gardens of Ingleborough Hall and the fantastic stalactites and stalagmites of Ingleborough Show Cave

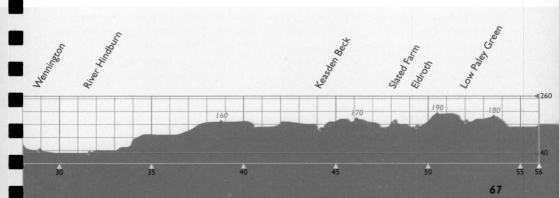

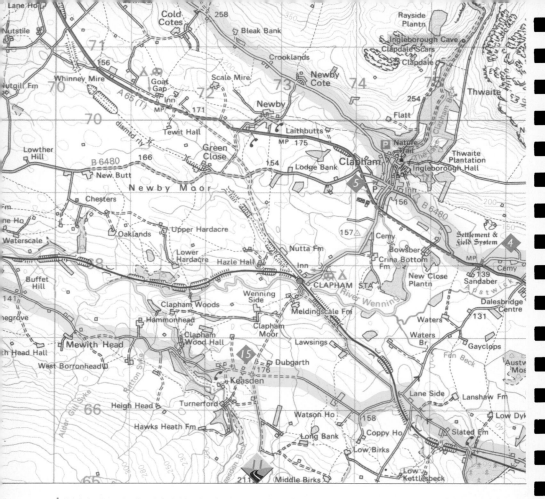

1 With back to the Royal Oak Hotel in Settle L out of town under railway bridge, over bridge and 1st R after swimming baths onto Stackhouse Lane 'Stackhouse 1, Little Stainforth 2'

2 Fine dry stone walling to the left! After 5 km (3½ miles) at X-roads by quarry L '7 ft 6 in width limit'

3 At T-j in Austwick shortly after Game Cock PH bear R (in effect SA) 'Clapham 1¾' (Or for short cut turn L 'Settle 4¾')

4 At T-j with A65 R 'Kendal', then shortly 1st R 'Clapham' (the A65 is a busy road – **take care**)

5 Into Clapham, follow the road over the bridge and take the 3rd R onto Cross Haw Lane by a large stone barn. (Or for second short cut, cross the bridge in

Clapham and immediately L onto Station Road 'Clapham Station, Slaidburn')

➡ page 70

15 At X-roads after 5 km (3½ miles) SA 'Settle 7¼' (Or for link to Route 11 turn R to join the other route at instruction 4 'Slaidburn 11½')

16 Follow this road for 6 km (4 miles) going beneath the railway line once and over it twice. At X-roads R 'Settle 2¾'

17 At X-roads with A65 SA '7.5 ton weight limit'

18 Follow road into Settle. At T-j at the end of Station Road L to return to the start

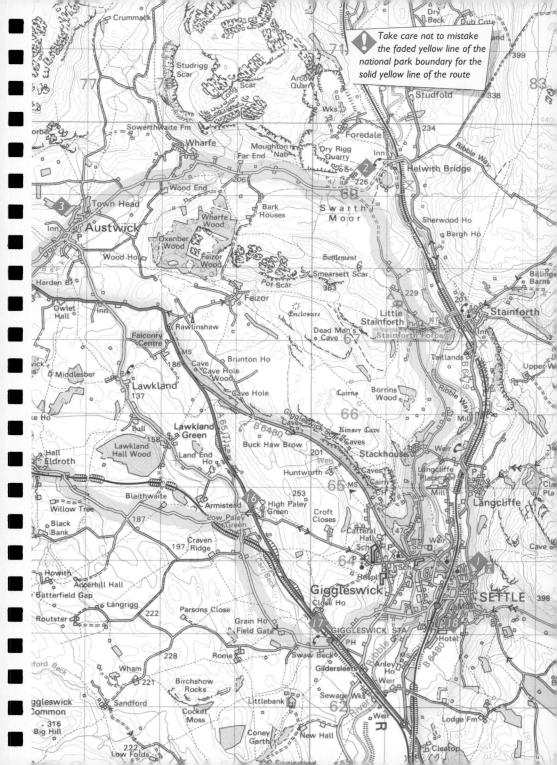

Take care not to mistake the faded yellow line of the national park boundary for the solid yellow line of the route

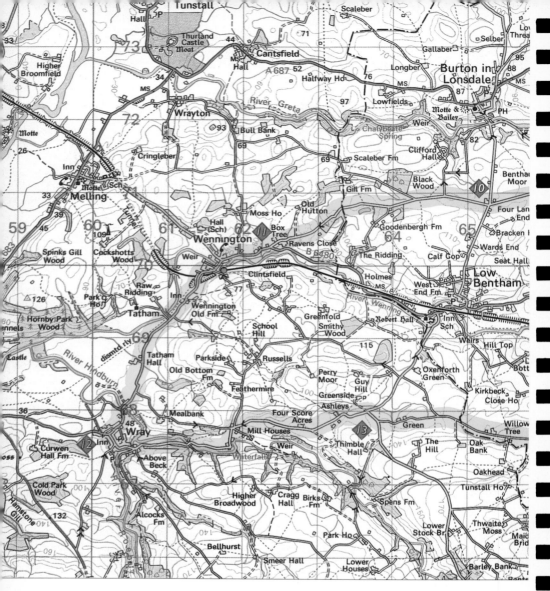

6 After 5 km (3½ miles) at T-j with B6255 L 'Ingleton ¼' then 3rd R 'Main car park, Tourist Information Centre'

7 Follow signs for village centre through car park. At T-j with the railway viaduct ahead·L for continuation of route. (**Or** turn R at T-j to visit Ingleton and/or link to Route 8 to join the other route at instruction 1)

8 Follow signs for Kendal. At T-j with A65 by Bridge Hotel R 'Kendal' then L on Bentham Road 'Bentham 3½'

9 Steep hill. Shortly after LH bend with a turning to Burton in Lonsdsale turn R at X-roads (your right of way) 'Wennington 3¼'

10 At X-roads SA 'Wennington 2¼'

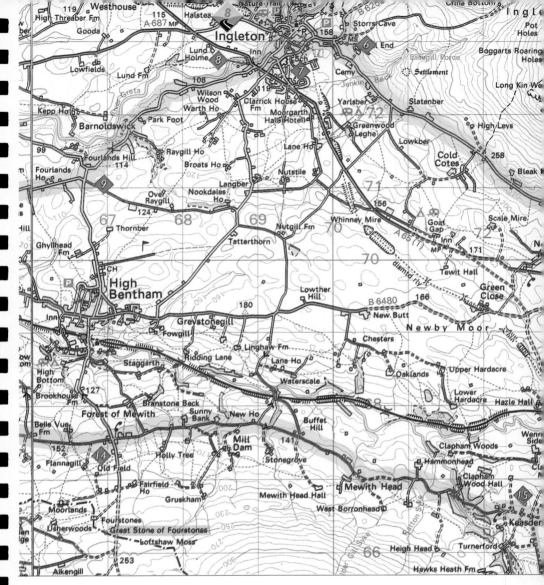

11 *After 3 km (2 miles) at T-j with B6480 R (NS)*

12 *Go through Wennington. After 3 km (2 miles) cross bridge over the River Hindburn, go into Wray and take 1st L 'Higher Tatham, Low Gill' towards the George & Dragon PH*

13 *Cross bridge, climb hill. 800 m (½ mile) after the start of descent 1st R by stone bus shelter 'Lowgill 2' then shortly 1st L 'Settle 12'*

14 *At X-roads SA 'Settle 10'*

15 *At X-roads after 5 km (3½ miles) SA 'Settle 7¼' (**Or** for link to Route 11 turn R to join the other route at instruction 4 'Slaidburn 11½')*

⬅ **page 68**

From Settle to Malham and along Littondale

Malham and Malham Cove are two of the honeypots of the Dales so be prepared for extra traffic and lots of people on the 3-km (2-mile) section from Kirby Malham to Malham itself. By contrast, Littondale is one of the quietest but loveliest dales in the region and makes for some gentle cycling along the valley bottom. Before all of this there is a savage climb to negotiate out of Settle. Try walking to leave yourself fresh for the rest of the ride – there are three more steep climbs to tackle. Littondale has the feel of a lost valley as it is not on the way to anywhere else. On reaching Halton Gill you face the final big climb alongside Pen-y-ghent. Having descended into the Ribble Valley, the busy B6479 is avoided by linking with the parallel back lane fom Little Stainforth to Settle.

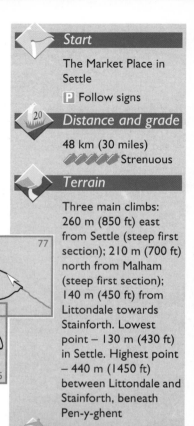

Start

The Market Place in Settle

P Follow signs

Distance and grade

48 km (30 miles)
Strenuous

Terrain

Three main climbs: 260 m (850 ft) east from Settle (steep first section); 210 m (700 ft) north from Malham (steep first section); 140 m (450 ft) from Littondale towards Stainforth. Lowest point – 130 m (430 ft) in Settle. Highest point – 440 m (1450 ft) between Littondale and Stainforth, beneath Pen-y-ghent

Nearest railway

Settle

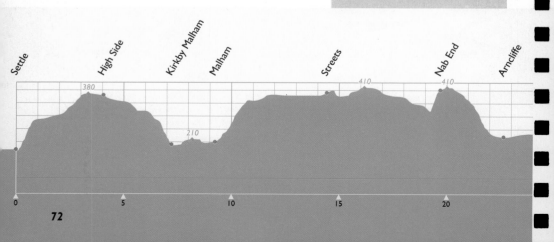

Langcliffe Scar 1
The craggy headlands of the scar are riddled with caves, the most famous of which is Victoria Cave. Relics from this and other caves are on display at the Pig Yard Museum in Settle

Refreshments

Royal Oak PH 🍴🍺, Golden Lion PH 🍺, **Settle**
Victoria PH 🍺, **Kirkby Malham**
Lister Arms 🍺, Buck PH 🍺, **Malham**
Falcon PH 🍺, Raikes Cottage
Tea Room, **Arncliffe**
Queens Arms 🍴🍺, **Litton**

Malham Cove 3
A gigantic natural amphitheatre with walls 70 m (240 ft) high, created by earth movements in the Ice Age. Paths lead to the staggering cliffs of Gordale Scar where waterfalls plunge into a ravine 75 m (250 ft) deep. A mile north of the cove is Malham Tarn, a large lake with abundant bird life, where Charles Kingsley set the opening scenes of *The Water Babies*

▼ Littondale

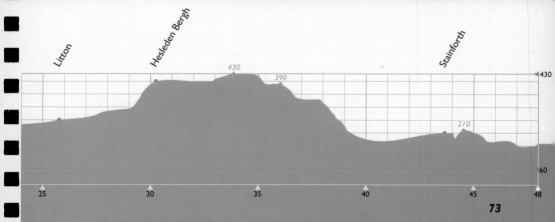

73

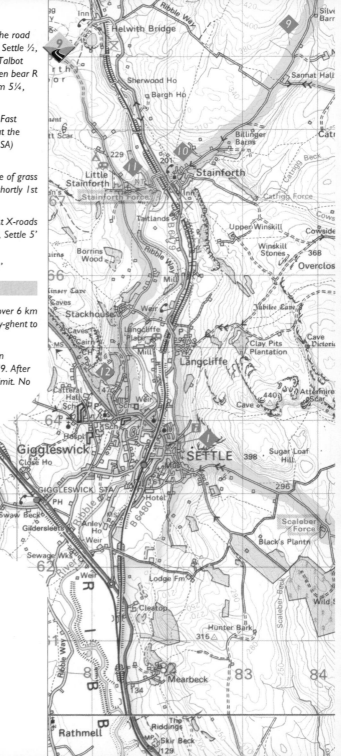

1 From the square in Settle take the road opposite the Royal Oak PH 'Upper Settle ½, Malham 6, Airton 6'. Go past the Talbot Arms. At T-j by the Post Office L then bear R onto Victoria Street 'Kirkby Malham 5¼, Airton 6¼'

2 Climb steeply then more gently. Fast descent. At T-j in Kirkby Malham at the bottom of the hill bear L (in effect SA) 'Malham 1½'

3 In Malham bear R at the triangle of grass 'Gordale 1, Malham Tarn 3' then shortly 1st L 'Malham Tarn 3'

4 Climb past car park to the tarn. At X-roads R 'Arncliffe 6' (**Or** SA 'Langcliffe 5, Settle 5' for short cut)

5 Shortly, at T-j bear R 'Arncliffe 5'

➤ page 76

9 Climb steeply then more gently over 6 km (4 miles) with the mountain of Pen-y-ghent to the right. Descend to Stainforth

10 At T-j in Stainforth R 'Horton in Ribblesdale' then R again on B6479. After 180 m (200 yd) 1st L '6 ft width limit. No access to caravan site'

11 Cross bridge, climb. At T-j just past caravan site L (NS) (**Or** for link to Route 9 turn R at T-j to join the other route at instructions 1/2)

12 On the outskirts of Settle, at T-j with A65 at the end of Stackhouse Lane L 'Settle, Skipton' to return to start

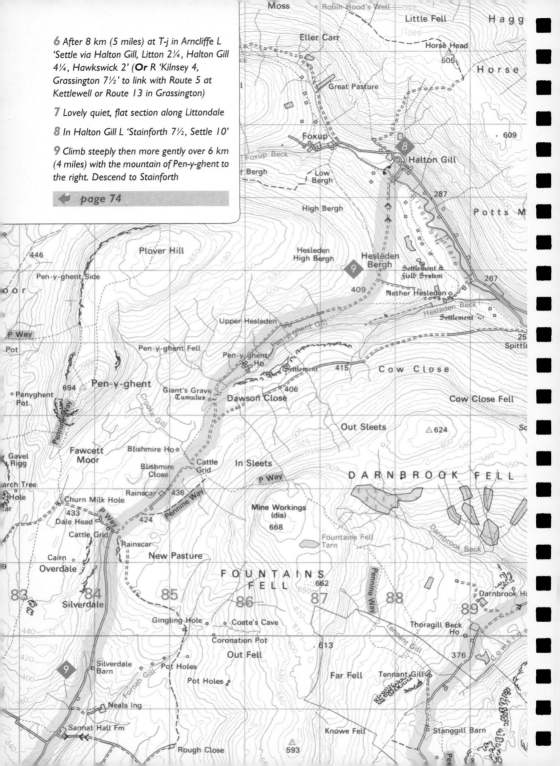

6 After 8 km (5 miles) at T-j in Arncliffe L 'Settle via Halton Gill, Litton 2¼, Halton Gill 4¼, Hawkswick 2' (**Or** R 'Kilnsey 4, Grassington 7½ to link with Route 5 at Kettlewell or Route 13 in Grassington)

7 Lovely quiet, flat section along Littondale

8 In Halton Gill L 'Stainforth 7½, Settle 10'

9 Climb steeply then more gently over 6 km (4 miles) with the mountain of Pen-y-ghent to the right. Descend to Stainforth

← page 74

Gisburn Forest and Bolton-by-Bowland

The third and last of the rides starting from Settle, explores the hills either side of the Ribble Valley with a short route option. West from Settle, the ride follows the River Wenning before cutting south at Keasden and climbing out of the valley of Keasden Beck to the high point at Bowland Knotts. A fast descent through Gisburn Forest and past Stocks Reservoir to the B6478 and the crossroads with three options: turn left to link to Route 12, starting from Slaidburn; right for a short cut to Settle or straight ahead for the full route through Bolton-by-Bowland and Hellifield. Views of Langcliffe Scar open up before the steep run down to the square in Settle.

turn left to link to Route 12

Start

The Golden Lion Hotel, near the Market Place, Settle

P Follow signs

Distance and grade

58 km (36 miles) — short route 40 km (25 miles)

🚴🚴🚴🚴🚴 Strenuous (short route: Moderate)

Terrain

Four main climbs: 275 m (900 ft) to Bowland Knotts from just beyond Eldroth; 85 m (280 ft) south from from Stocks Reservoir; 100 m (350 ft) northeast from Bolton-by-Bowland; 210 m (700 ft) from Airton to High Side (avoided by short cut). Lowest point – 90 m

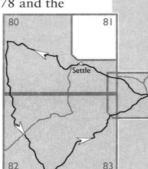

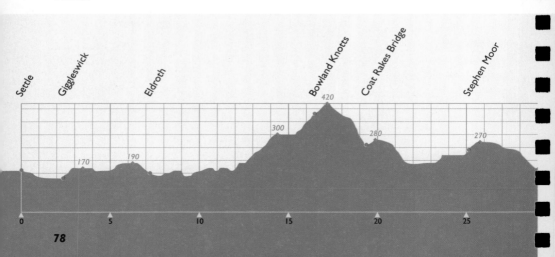

(290 ft) at Bolton-by-Bowland. Highest point – 420 m (1390 ft) at Bowland Knotts

Nearest railway

Settle

▲ Bolton-by-Bowland

Places of interest

Bowland Knotts *4/5*
Dark crags tower above the moorland, Gisburn Forest and Stocks Reservoir. There are views across to the limestone peaks of Whernside, Ingleborough and Pen-y-Ghent

Bolton-by-Bowland *7*
An attractive village of whitewashed houses and two tree-fringed greens by Tosside Beck. The Medieval Church of St Peter and St Paul has a memorial to the 15th-century landowner Sir Ralph Pudsey, his three wives and 25 children

Refreshments

Royal Oak PH ♟♟, *Golden Lion PH* ♟, **Settle**
Copy Nook Hotel, Coach & Horses PH ♟,
Bolton-by-Bowland
Black Horse PH, **Hellifield**
Plough Inn ♟♟, **Wigglesworth**
(on short cut)

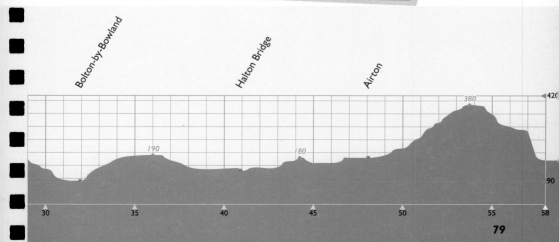

1 With back to the Golden Lion Hotel in Settle L then 1st R onto Station Road 'Station, Sowarth Industrial Estate'

2 Follow signs for Lawkland and Giggleswick Station. At X-roads with A65 SA beneath railway bridge (NS)

3 Ignore 1st left ('Single track road'). Shortly after crossing bridge over railway take next L at X-roads (your right of way) 'Eldroth 2'

4 Follow signs for Bentham and Slaidburn. At X-roads after 9 km (5½ miles) L 'Slaidburn 11½'

➡ **page 83**

9 At T-j with the busy A65 R 'Skipton' then after ½ mile, at the end of the village bear L 'Airton 3½, Malham 6'

10 At X-roads in Airton L 'Kirkby Malham 1½, Malham 2½' then after 270 m (300 yd) 1st L by triangle of grass and wooden bench 'Settle 6¼' (**For link** to Route 10 turn L at X-roads in Airton then go straight ahead into Kirkby Malham to join the other route at instructions 2/3)

11 Climb steadily over 5 km (3 miles). At T-j bear L (in effect SA) 'Settle 3¼'

12 Steady then steep descent. On LH bend shortly after cobbled section at the start of Settle R past Post Office and Talbot Inn to return to the square

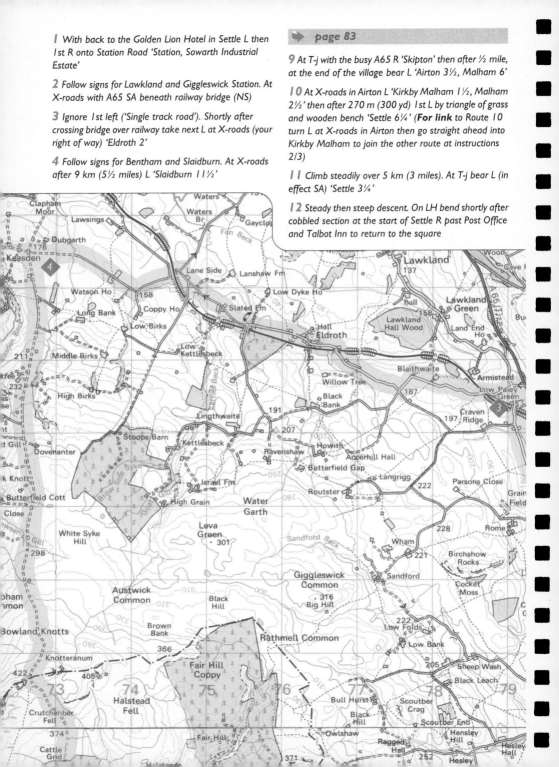

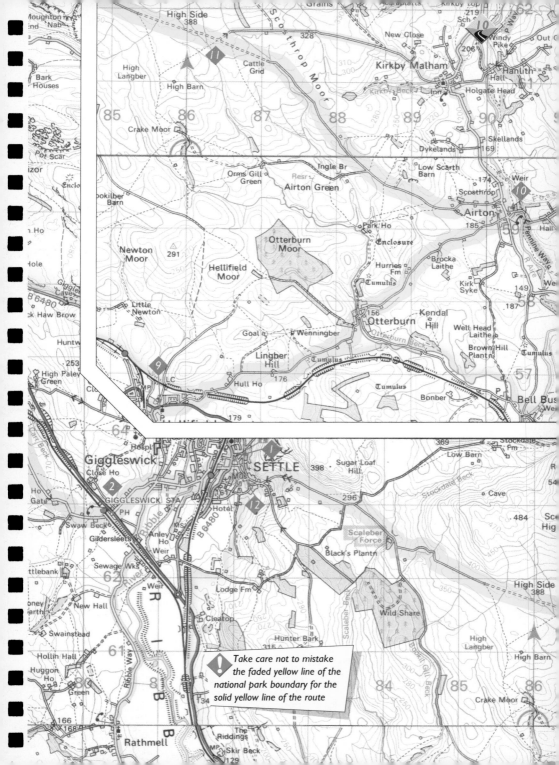

Take care not to mistake the faded yellow line of the national park boundary for the solid yellow line of the route

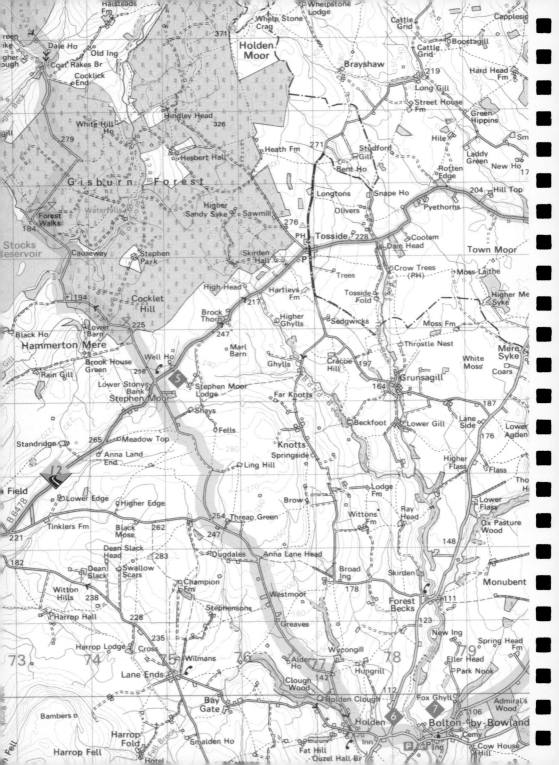

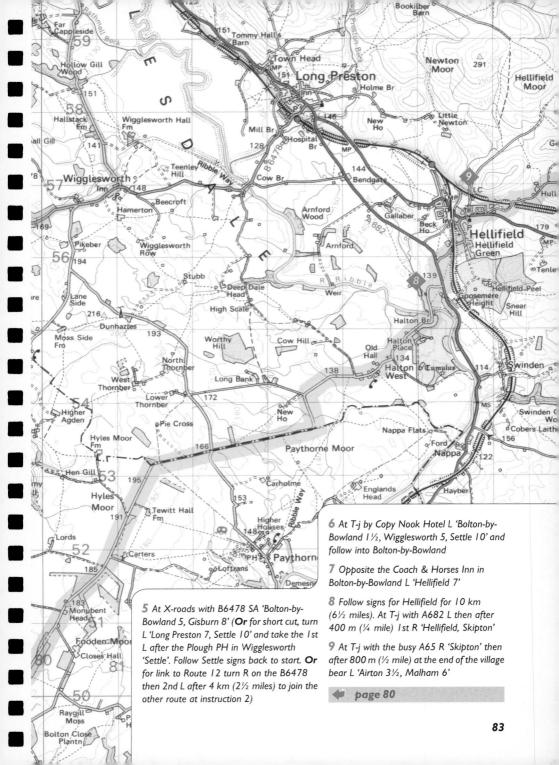

5 At X-roads with B6478 SA 'Bolton-by-Bowland 5, Gisburn 8' (**Or** for short cut, turn L 'Long Preston 7, Settle 10' and take the 1st L after the Plough PH in Wigglesworth 'Settle'. Follow Settle signs back to start. **Or** for link to Route 12 turn R on the B6478 then 2nd L after 4 km (2½ miles) to join the other route at instruction 2)

6 At T-j by Copy Nook Hotel L 'Bolton-by-Bowland 1½, Wigglesworth 5, Settle 10' and follow into Bolton-by-Bowland

7 Opposite the Coach & Horses Inn in Bolton-by-Bowland L 'Hellifield 7'

8 Follow signs for Hellifield for 10 km (6½ miles). At T-j with A682 L then after 400 m (¼ mile) 1st R 'Hellifield, Skipton'

9 At T-j with the busy A65 R 'Skipton' then after 800 m (½ mile) at the end of the village bear L 'Airton 3½, Malham 6'

◀ page 80

Slaidburn and the Trough of Bowland

12

The Yorkshire Dales can get very busy in the summer and even the small lanes can fill up with cars. The Forest of Bowland in Lancashire is a lot less well-known and offers a quieter option. A short section of Roman road is followed either side of Cow Ark. Chipping is a charming village and with Oakenclough, some 11 km (7 miles) further on, offers the only pub stop until almost the end of the ride. To the west of the fells of the Forest of Bowland there are views out to sea in Morecambe Bay.

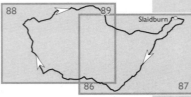

The ride then turns east and enters the Trough of Bowland – a narrow valley that climbs through pine woodland up to the pass. Three rivers meet near Dunsop Bridge and it is the River Hodder that is followed from Dunsop Bridge through Newton and back to the start.

Start

The car park in Slaidburn

P As above

Distance and grade

56 km (35 miles)

Moderate/strenuous

Terrain

Three main climbs: 150 m (500 ft) towards Cow Ark; 130 m (430 ft) northwest from Chipping; 210 m (700 ft) from instruction 12 to the pass through the Trough of Bowland. Lowest point – 80 m (260 ft) at instruction 12. Highest point – 300 m 980 feet) through the Trough of Bowland

Nearest railway

Clitheroe, 10 km (6 miles) southeast of the route at Cow Ark (instruction 4)

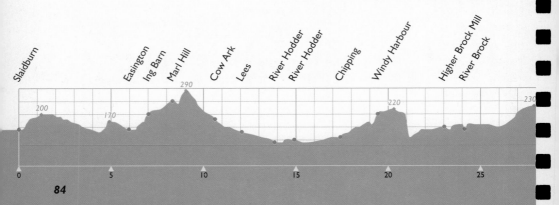

Slaidburn 1

Coiling up over the fells around Slaidburn are wild and deserted salt tracks – Salter Fell, Higher Salter Close, High Salter. The latter leads on to Hornby Castle, over the River Lune, to Gressingham. Pack ponies would follow these regonised saltways from Cheshire, south Lancashire, or the coastal salt pans – salt was the only way of preserving meat during the winter and each farm needed plenty of it

Chipping 7

Charming village of cobbled pavements and 17th-century houses above a fast-flowing stream. St Bartholomew's Church has a tower dating back to 1450 and examples of the chair-making craft for which the village is justly famed

◄ Marshaw Wyre, Trough of Bowland

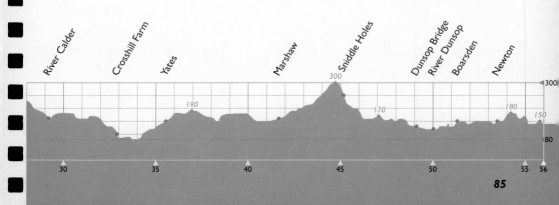

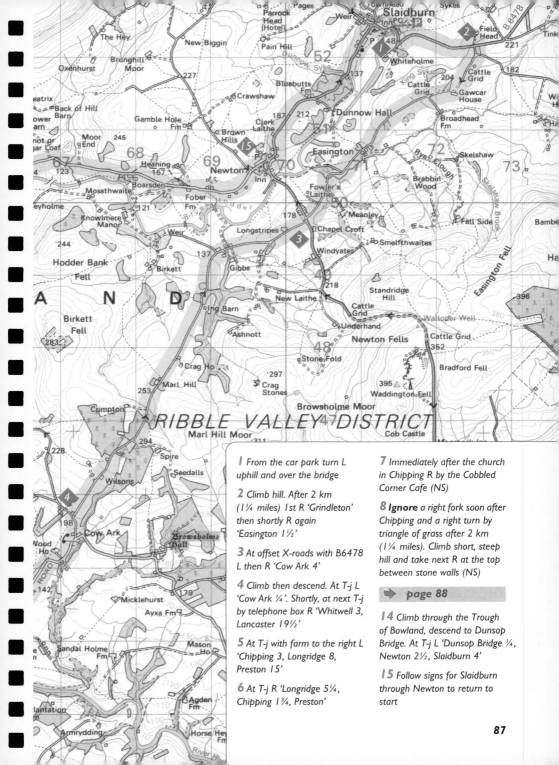

1 From the car park turn L uphill and over the bridge

2 Climb hill. After 2 km (1¼ miles) 1st R 'Grindleton' then shortly R again 'Easington 1½'

3 At offset X-roads with B6478 L then R 'Cow Ark 4'

4 Climb then descend. At T-j L 'Cow Ark ¼'. Shortly, at next T-j by telephone box R 'Whitwell 3, Lancaster 19½'

5 At T-j with farm to the right L 'Chipping 3, Longridge 8, Preston 15'

6 At T-j R 'Longridge 5¼, Chipping 1¾, Preston'

7 Immediately after the church in Chipping R by the Cobbled Corner Cafe (NS)

8 **Ignore** a right fork soon after Chipping and a right turn by triangle of grass after 2 km (1¼ miles). Climb short, steep hill and take next R at the top between stone walls (NS)

➡ *page 88*

14 Climb through the Trough of Bowland, descend to Dunsop Bridge. At T-j L 'Dunsop Bridge ¼, Newton 2½, Slaidburn 4'

15 Follow signs for Slaidburn through Newton to return to start

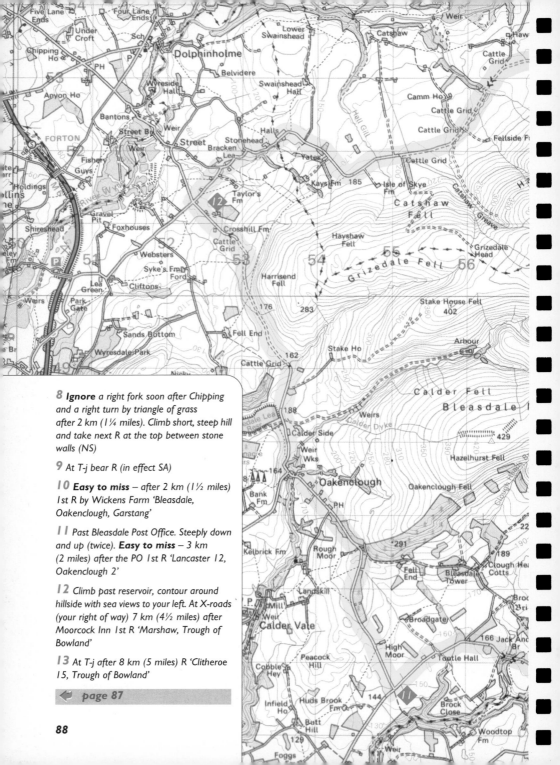

8 Ignore a right fork soon after Chipping and a right turn by triangle of grass after 2 km (1¼ miles). Climb short, steep hill and take next R at the top between stone walls (NS)

9 At T-j bear R (in effect SA)

10 Easy to miss – after 2 km (1½ miles) 1st R by Wickens Farm 'Bleasdale, Oakenclough, Garstang'

11 Past Bleasdale Post Office. Steeply down and up (twice). **Easy to miss** – 3 km (2 miles) after the PO 1st R 'Lancaster 12, Oakenclough 2'

12 Climb past reservoir, contour around hillside with sea views to your left. At X-roads (your right of way) 7 km (4½ miles) after Moorcock Inn 1st R 'Marshaw, Trough of Bowland'

13 At T-j after 8 km (5 miles) R 'Clitheroe 15, Trough of Bowland'

◀ page 87

From Skipton to Grassington

After leaving Skipton the route passes through the delights of Wharfedale, Bolton Abbey (if you choose to make the diversion), the old hunting lodge of Barden Tower and the River Wharfe as it cuts through the splendid limestone scenery. After the diversions of Grassington and Linton there is a short stretch on the busy B6265 before turning off to Hetton and Gargrave. The climb up onto the crossroads between Broughton and Carleton is rewarded with wide views of the hills that tower over Grassington before a long descent through Carleton back to Skipton.

 Start

Black Horse Hotel at the roundabout at the end of the High Street, Skipton

P Follow signs

 Distance and grade

45 km (28 miles)
Moderate

 Terrain

Two main climbs: 210 m (700 ft) from Skipton to Halton Height; 180 m (600 ft) between Broughton and Carleton. Lowest point – 90 m (300 ft) at crossing of the River Aire. Highest point – 315 m (1030 ft) at Halton Height

 Nearest railway

Skipton

Refreshments

Black Horse PH 🍺, Royal Shepherd PH 🍺, **Skipton**
Elm Tree Inn 🍺, **Embsay**
New Inn 🍺, Craven Arms 🍺🍺, **Appletreewick**
Black Horse PH 🍺, Devonshire PH 🍺, **Grassington**   Fountaine Inn 🍺🍺, **Linton**
Devonshire Arms 🍺🍺, Cracoe Cafe, **Cracoe**
Angel Inn 🍺🍺, **Hetton**
Old Swan PH, Masons Arms 🍺, **Gargrave**

▶ Wharfedale and Appletreewick

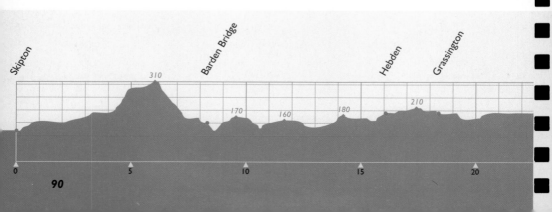

Skipton 1
Two massive stone towers guard the entrance to Skipton Castle – a moated fort boasting a 15 m (50 ft) long banqueting hall, a 'shell room' with walls decorated with seashells, a large kitchen and a dungeon

Barden Tower 5
The picturesque ruins of Barden Tower, a 15th-century hunting lodge, were restored by Lady Anne Clifford in 1659

Appletreewick 6/7
Pretty hillside village with old merchants' and yeoman farmers' houses and cottages together with the fine 17th-century mansions of Mock Beggar Hall and High Hall.

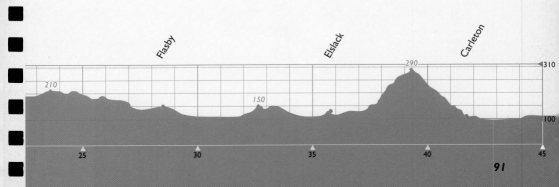

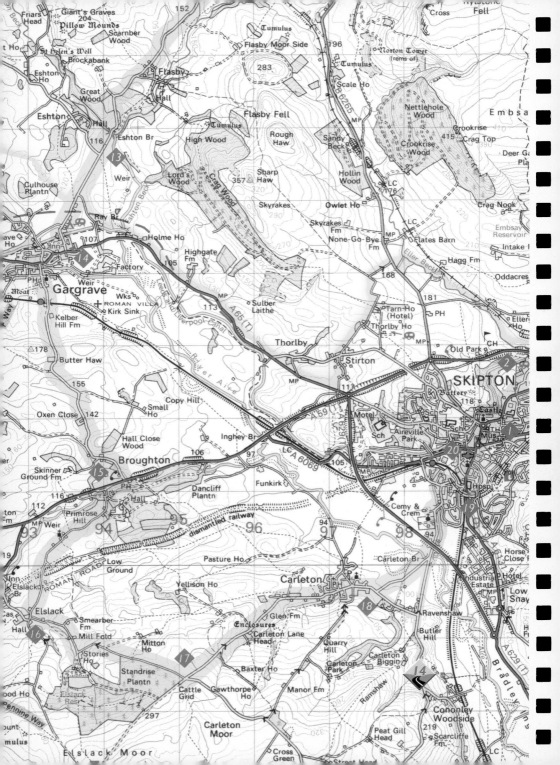

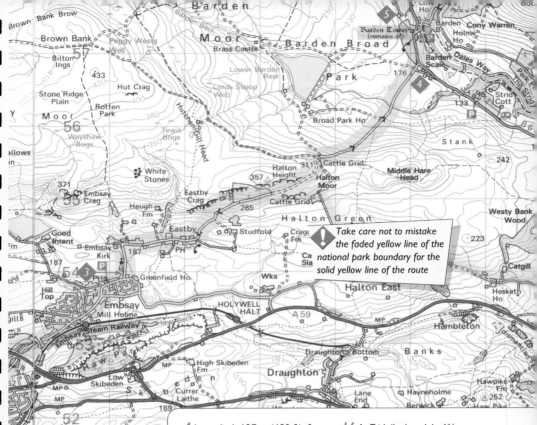

Take care not to mistake the faded yellow line of the national park boundary for the solid yellow line of the route

1 With back to the Black Horse Hotel L take the Harrogate (A59) road at the roundabout 'Embsay 1¾, Eastby 2½, Bolton Abbey 6'

2 Go past the castle, climb the hill then 1st L 'Embsay 1¼, Eastby 2'

3 Through Embsay. 270 m (300 yd) past the Elm Tree Inn and car park on your left 1st L on Kirk Lane 'Eastby ¾, Barden 3½, Pateley Bridge 14' (**Or** if you wish to visit Bolton Abbey, do not turn left on Kirk Lane but follow this road for 8 km (5 miles) passing through Halton East. At the B6160 (site of Bolton Abbey) turn L for 5 km (3 miles) and rejoin the route at instruction 5 '...immediately after...')

4 Long climb 137 m (450 ft), fast descent. At T-j with B6160 after 5 km (3½ miles) L 'Burnsall 3¼, Grassington 6½'

5 After 800 m (½ mile) and immediately after the remains of Barden Tower R 'Appletreewick 2½, Pateley Bridge 10'

➡ page 94

13 At T-j bear L 'Gargrave 1¼, Skipton 5, Settle 12'

14 At T-j with A65 in Gargrave R 'Settle, Kendal' then shortly after Old Swan PH on the right and telephone box on the left, next L over bridge 'Broughton 2'

15 At T-j with A59 by the Bull Inn R 'Clitheroe' then 1st L onto slip road. At T-j L again over bridge

16 At T-j L 'Lothersdale 4¾, Crosshills 6'

17 Climb. Fabulous views to the left. At X-roads L 'Carleton 1½, Skipton 3½'

18 Fast descent. (**For link** to Route 14, 800 m (½ mile) after Swan PH in Carleton on sharp LH bend 1st R 'Cononley, Lothersdale' then at T-j at the end of Carla Beck Lane R (same sign) to link at instructions 3/4)

19 At T-j at the end of Carleton Road just after bridge over railway L 'Town Centre'

20 Cross canal. At mini-roundabout bear L to return to start

4 Long climb 140 m (450 ft), fast descent. At T-j with B6160 after 5 km (3½ miles) L 'Burnsall 3¼, Grassington 6½'

5 After 800 m (½ mile) and immediately after the remains of Barden Tower R 'Appletreewick 2½, Pateley Bridge 10'

6 At T-j after 3 km (2 miles) L 'Appletreewick ¼'

7 After 2 km (1½ miles) and shortly after crossing bridge over stream 1st R 'Hartlington Raikes, Hebden 2' then 1st L 'Hebden 1¾'

8 At T-j with B6265 by the Clarendon Hotel L (NS)

9 Into Grassington. Turn R for the village centre or SA for continuation of route. (**Or** for link to Settle and Wensleydale routes turn next R 'Conistone, Kettlewell'. For Settle routes (9, 10, 11) follow signs for Arncliffe. For Wensleydale routes (3, 4, 5) follow signs for Kettlewell)

10 From Grassington take the B6265 towards Threshfield. Cross bridge and 1st L 'Linton ¾, Burnsall 3'. At X-roads with B6160 SA onto B6265 'Linton ¼, Cracoe 2½, Skipton 9'

11 At T-j near quarry L (NS). **Busy** 3-km (2-mile) section

12 400 m (¼ mile) after the Devonshire Arms PH in Cracoe 1st R 'Hetton 1, Gargrave 5'

◀ page 93

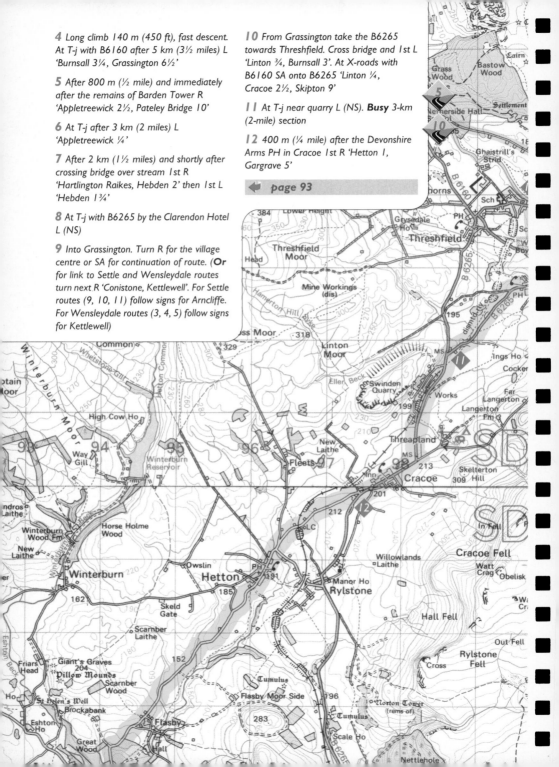

From Skipton to Ilkley Moor and Bolton Abbey

14

After crossing the railway and the River Aire near to Cononley the route stays on the north side of Airedale, above the Leeds and Liverpool Canal. A steep climb after Silsden takes you higher up the hillside almost 180 m

Distance and grade

42 km (26 miles)
Moderate

▼ Bolton Abbey

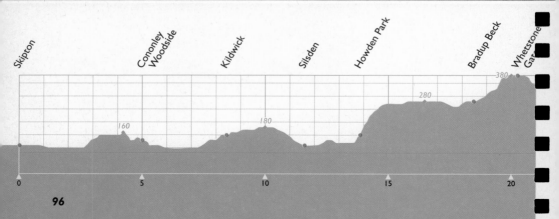

96

Terrain

Two main climbs:
270 m (900 ft) from
Silsden; 100 m (350 ft)
from Bolton to Halton
East. Lowest point –
80 m (260 feet) in Ilkley.
Highest point – 365 m
(1200 ft) at the masts
above Ilkley

Nearest railway

Skipton

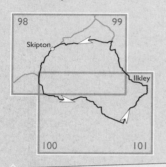

Refreshments

Black Horse PH 🍺, Royal Shepherd PH 🍺,
Skipton   New Inn, Railway PH, **Cononley**
Plenty of choice in **Silsden**
Plenty of choice in **Ilkley**
Forge Cafe, Bolton Abbey Tea Shop,
Devonshire Arms Hotel, **Bolton Abbey**

(600 ft) above the valley floor. The crossing of Ilkley Moor, via the masts at the top, involves a short, rough section of unsealed road and you may have to dismount for a short section on the descent – particularly if you are on a light, road bike. Gravity helps you cross quickly through the built-up area around Ilkley and you soon join a quiet lane on the north side of the River Wharfe. Bolton Abbey is well worth a visit, for its setting as much as anything else. Quiet lanes westwards through Halton East take you back to Embsay and Skipton.

Places of interest

Ilkley *12*
A Roman fort that became an elegant 19th-century spa town and a retreat for wealthy Bradford wool merchants. The Elizabethan Manor House Museum and Art Gallery, on the site of the Roman fort and near an exposed section of Roman wall, tells the history of the town

Bolton Abbey *16*
The charming ruins of the 12th-century Augustinian priory are set among woods, waterfalls and meadows. Eleven paintings on the east wall symbolise the life of Christ

1 From the roundabout with the winged statue at the end of the High Street in Skipton take the road signposted 'Clitheroe, Burnley, Bradford'

2 At mini-roundabout at the end of High Street bear R past bus station. Over the canal. Immediately after petrol station (and before going under railway bridge) R onto Carleton Road 'Carleton 1½, Lothersdale 4½'

3 Shortly after going under flyover, on sharp RH bend bear L (in effect SA) (NS). Follow signs for Cononley

➡ *page 100*

14 After 5 km (3 miles) at T-j by triangle of grass R 'Beamsley 1¾'

15 At T-j with the horrendous A59 L onto cycleway/footpath running parallel with main road. Follow it underneath the road bridge to emerge at old river bridge. Turn L then at T-j (with B6160) by the Forge Cafe and Devonshire Arms Hotel turn R

16 Shortly after passing the car park for Bolton Abbey on your left next L by triangle of grass (NS). (**Or** for link to Route 13 do not turn left but continue SA, joining other route at instructions 4/5)

17 Through Halton East. **Ignore** two left turns, the first signposted 'Skipton 4' and the second at a X-roads with quarry works to the right. Shortly after a sharp RH bend take the next L by triangle of grass into Embsay 'Skipton 2'

18 At T-j at the end of Shires Lane L 'Dales Railway'

19 At T-j with A59 R 'Skipton' to return to the start

⚠ Take care not to mistake the faded yellow line of the national park boundary for the solid yellow line of the route

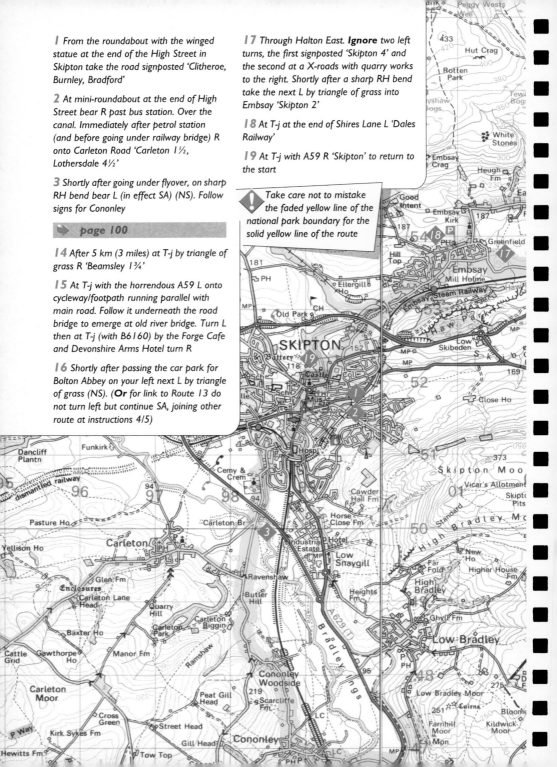

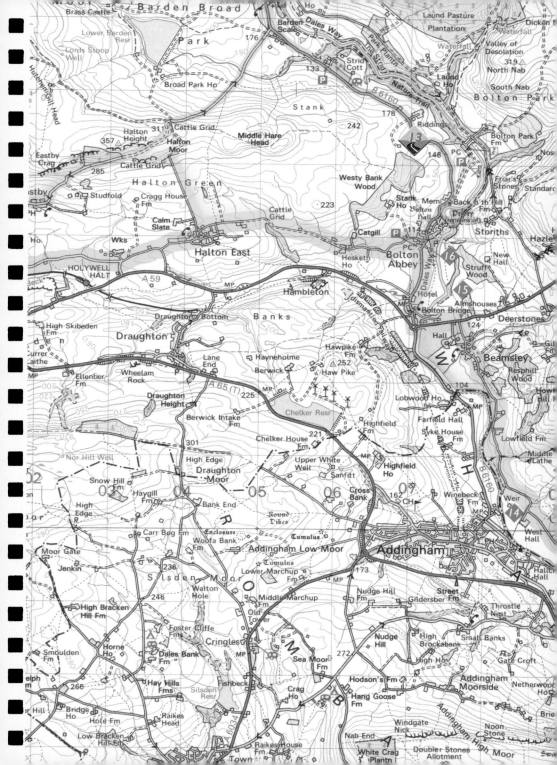

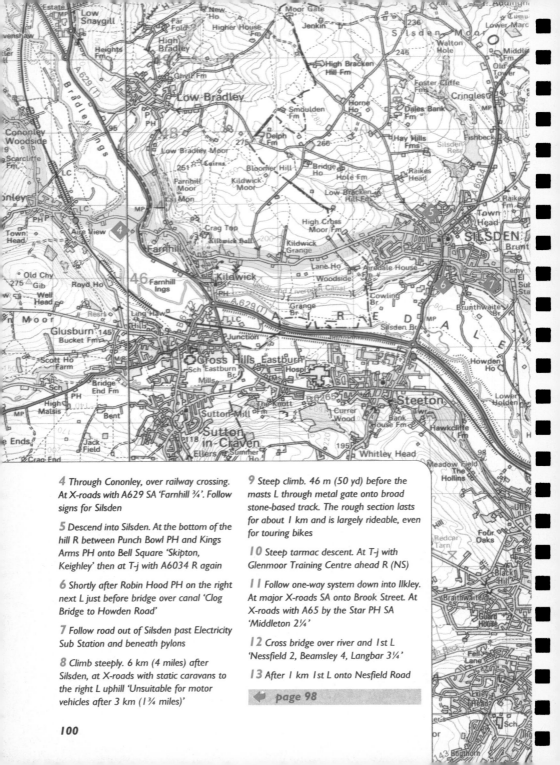

4 Through Cononley, over railway crossing. At X-roads with A629 SA 'Farnhill ¾'. Follow signs for Silsden

5 Descend into Silsden. At the bottom of the hill R between Punch Bowl PH and Kings Arms PH onto Bell Square 'Skipton, Keighley' then at T-j with A6034 R again

6 Shortly after Robin Hood PH on the right next L just before bridge over canal 'Clog Bridge to Howden Road'

7 Follow road out of Silsden past Electricity Sub Station and beneath pylons

8 Climb steeply. 6 km (4 miles) after Silsden, at X-roads with static caravans to the right L uphill 'Unsuitable for motor vehicles after 3 km (1¾ miles)'

9 Steep climb. 46 m (50 yd) before the masts L through metal gate onto broad stone-based track. The rough section lasts for about 1 km and is largely rideable, even for touring bikes

10 Steep tarmac descent. At T-j with Glenmoor Training Centre ahead R (NS)

11 Follow one-way system down into Ilkley. At major X-roads SA onto Brook Street. At X-roads with A65 by the Star PH SA 'Middleton 2¼'

12 Cross bridge over river and 1st L 'Nessfield 2, Beamsley 4, Langbar 3¼'

13 After 1 km 1st L onto Nesfield Road

◀ page 98

Along the River Swale to Keld

The westernmost of the four routes starting in Swaledale, this short ride starts in the small village of Muker and heads east down the main valley road through Swaledale. After cutting north on a minor lane to cross the River Swale then swinging west, above the valley, the route turns to track and descends alongside the river for one of the most delightful stretches of riverside riding in all the Dales. Soon after passing the old lead-mining ruins you are faced with a choice: in the summer and autumn, when the trail has dried out, it is possible to continue north on the course of the Pennine Way along the valley of Stonesdale Beck (parts of this are quite rough); otherwise it is suggested you cross the River Swale, just beyond the waterfalls of Kisdon Gorge, into the hamlet of Keld. The final climb, up onto Kisdon Hill, is the steepest of the day but it is followed by the best views and the best downhill stretch, back to the start.

Start

The pay and display car park on the B6270 on the eastern edge of Muker

P As above

Distance and grade

21 km (13 miles) – short route 14 km (9 miles)

///// Moderate/ strenuous

Terrain

Riverside track through Swaledale, broadleaf woodland and moorland. Three main climbs: 110 m (360 ft) after crossing the River Swale; 140 m (460 ft) along the Pennine Way north from Keld; 170 m (570 ft) over Kisdon Hill. Lowest point – 230 m (755 ft) at the crossing of the River

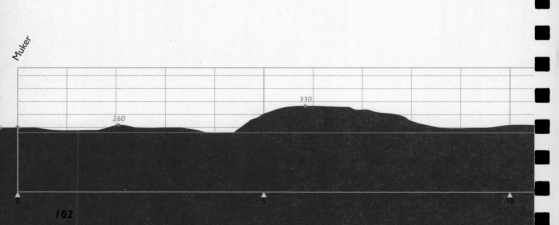

Swale. Highest point —
490 m (1610 ft) at the
top of Kisdon Hill

Nearest railway

Garsdale Head, 19 km
(12 miles) southwest of
Muker

▼ *The River Swale near Muker*

Places of interest

Muker 1
Pronounced 'Mewker' and meaning
'narrow field', the village has one of Britain's
few parish churches built in the reign of
Elizabeth I. Originally thatched with
heather, it was welcomed by the poor
Dalesfolk who, to bury their dead in
consecrated ground, previously had to
carry bodies in wicker coffins to Grinton,
16 km (10 miles) to the east. The
path the mourners took is the
bridleway over Kisdon Hill

Kisdon Gorge 7
The noisy River Swale tumbles
through this thickly wooded glen
near the granite hamlet of Keld

Keld 8
Originally a Viking settlement, its
name comes from an old Norse
word for a well or spring. The
village today consists of a few
cottages and farm buildings, a hall
and chapel, all round or near a
rustic square flanked by the River
Swale

Refreshments

Farmers Arms 🍴🍴, tea rooms, **Muker**

[Elevation profile chart showing:]

Kisdon Force

Hooker Mill Scar

480

410

360

340

480

230

15   20   21

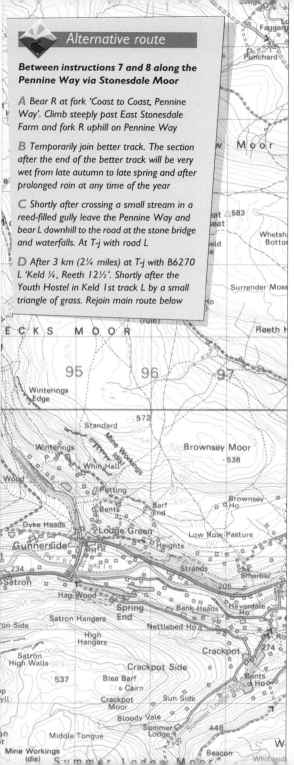

1 From the car park in Muker take the B6270 east towards Reeth

2 After 3 km (2 miles) take the 1st road L. Cross the bridge, climb steeply past telephone box

3 At the brow of the steep hill, just before a descent to a stone bridge ahead, turn L onto No Through Road

4 At fork of tarmac lanes stay on the upper RH fork

5 At the fork at the end of the tarmac section bear R on the upper track then follow the main stone track as it descends to the river

6 Lovely river section. Beyond the old mill ruins the track climbs steeply

7 Cross the stream (Catrake Force). At fork bear L 'Pennine Way, Keld' (**Or** SA for alternative route). Descend to cross river and bear R uphill. At the square in Keld L

8 At fork L, at T-j with main road L. After 400 m (¼ mile) 1st track L by small triangle of grass

9 Very steep climb. Superb grassy track with fine views

10 Very steep descent. At T-j with B6270 R to return to car park

From Feetham through mining ruins on Melbecks Moor

A short, rough walking section in the middle of the ride at the top end of Gunnerside Gill links two long stretches of excellent quality track through a landscape of old mining ruins, dotted all over Melbecks Moor and on

 Start

The Punchbowl PH in Feetham, on the B6270 west of Reeth

P Parking below the church or the lay-by opposite and the Punchbowl PH in Feetham

 Distance and grade

17 km (11 miles)
Strenuous

Terrain

Fine stone tracks over moorland through mining ruins; one rough, bouldery section at the start of Gunnerside Gill. Two climbs: 340 m (1115 ft) over 5 km (3½ miles) from Feetham (very steep near the start); 160 m (525 ft) from Gunnerside to Low Row Pasture. Lowest point – 230 m (755 ft)

▼ Swaledale near Gunnerside

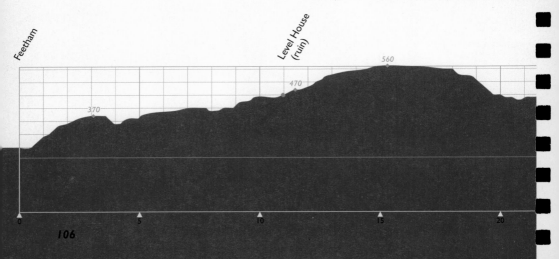

at the start. Highest
point – 570 m (1870 ft)
at the top of Melbecks
Moor

Nearest railway

Garsdale Head, 24 km
(15 miles) southwest of
the route at
Gunnerside

Places of interest

Gunnerside 9
The Norsemen gave Gunnerside its name –
it means gunnar's or warrior's pasture.
Some of the local farmhouses are built in
the style of Norse long-houses – reminders
of the first inhabitants who arrived in the
early 10th century. Lead has been mined
since Roman times and at the beginning of
the last century as many as 2000 men and
boys worked in the industry centred
around Gunnerside

Refreshments

*Punch Bowl Inn 🍴, **Feetham**
Kings Head PH, tearooms,
Gunnerside*

the hillsides of the valley formed by
Gunnerside Gill. A steep climb on tarmac out
of Swaledale drops you into the valley of
Barney Beck which is followed past the old
spoil heaps of the mining operations, now a
carpet of heather. The descent down to
Gunnerside Gill and the kilometre that
follows is a push on a narrow, bouldery track
but the going soon improves by a series of
impressive stone arches at the confluence of
two streams. A short
climb sets you up for a
magnificent descent along
the fern- and heather-clad
hillside down into
Gunnerside. Here you can
follow the B6270 along
Swaledale back to the start
or climb steeply up onto Low
Row Pasture for wide views
of Swaledale before a fast
tarmac descent back to the
start.

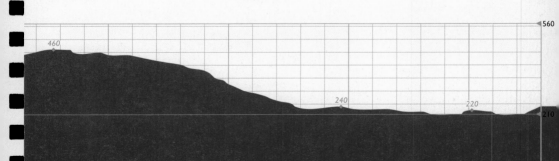

1 With back to the Punchbowl Inn L then 1st road L 'Langthwaite 3½'

2 Steep climb. Go over the brow of the hill, cross bridge over stream then 1st track L sharply back on yourself 'Bridleway, No vehicles'

3 Fine track by the river and the ruins of the Old Gang Lead Smelting Mill. At the 1st fork where the LH track dips to cross stream towards spoil heap bear R

4 At the next fork by a stone bridge bear L on the steeper of the two uphill tracks

5 Keep bearing R over this 'moonscape', past the cairn marking the summit, past a 'Footpath to Keld' sign to the left and follow the main track as it swings R (north) above the valley

6 **Easy to miss.** Just before the house bear L downhill off the main track onto a small indistinct track which cuts down across the hillside towards the bottom of the valley. (You will probably have to walk this and the next section). Near the bottom, at a T-j with a clearer path turn sharply L to follow the stream on its descent

7 At first set of ruins cross stream from left bank to right bank. The track improves dramatically by the junction of river valleys at the next set of ruins with its unusual round arches

8 Climb, then a fantastic long descent. At T-j with lane L

9 At X-roads with the B6270 in Gunnerside SA past the Kings Head PH 'Reeth 6, Richmond 17'. After 180 m (200 yd) at the end of the village bear L onto steep No Through Road 'Unsuitable for motors'

10 Steep 150-m (500-ft) climb. Fine views from the top. Track turns to tarmac. Fast descent back to the church and starting point in Feetham

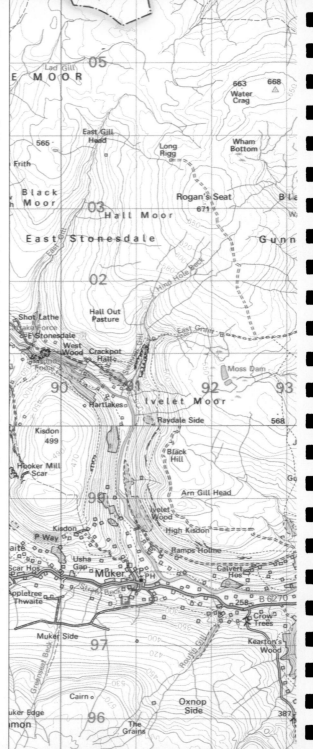

3 From Reeth, over Marrick Moor and Hurst Moor

Two off-road routes start from Reeth, this one heads north over Marrick Moor. The ride crosses Arkle Beck and climbs steeply from Fremington across the face of Fremington Edge. The views opening up behind are always a good excuse to stop on the way up the escarpment! After a short descent on tarmac to cross Shaw Beck and Skegdale Beck, the route goes off-road once again to climb to the highest point of the ride, on Moresdale Ridge. A steep, grassy descent leads down to the improbably named hamlet of Booze and to the refreshment stop at Langthwaite. From here you can follow the lane down Arkengarthdale back to Reeth or, alternatively, stay on the north side of the river which involves a rough middle section of almost 3 km (2 miles). The track improves close to Fremington and the outward route is rejoined to return to the start.

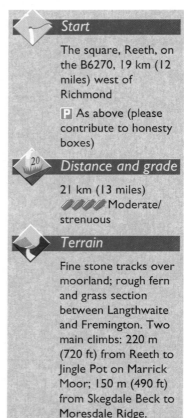

Start

The square, Reeth, on the B6270, 19 km (12 miles) west of Richmond

P As above (please contribute to honesty boxes)

Distance and grade

21 km (13 miles)
Moderate/ strenuous

Terrain

Fine stone tracks over moorland; rough fern and grass section between Langthwaite and Fremington. Two main climbs: 220 m (720 ft) from Reeth to Jingle Pot on Marrick Moor; 150 m (490 ft) from Skegdale Beck to Moresdale Ridge. Lowest point – 180 m (590 ft) at the crossing of Arkle Beck at the start. Highest point – 460 m (1510 ft) on Moresdale Ridge

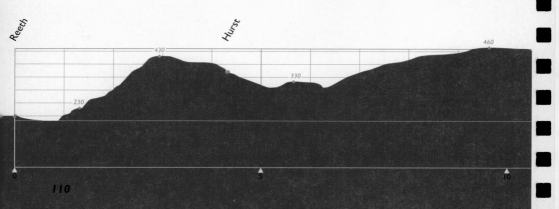

Nearest railway

Garsdale Head, 32 km (20 miles) west of Reeth

Refreshments

Black Bull PH 🍺, Kings Arms 🍺, plenty of choice in **Reeth** Red Lion PH 🍺, **Langthwaite**

Places of interest

Reeth 1

An imposing village, set at the junction of Swaledale and Arkengarthdale with a large, sloping village green and solid Georgian houses. The view from the green, looking down the valley towards Grinton and Fremington Edge, is magnificent. The green once held no fewer than seven fairs a year together with a weekly market. The fairs declined with the collapse of the lead mining industry by the 1860s and the population fell by two thirds

▼ Near Reeth

Langthwaite

Fremington

1 From the square in Reeth follow the B6270 downhill towards Leyburn and Richmond. Cross the bridge over Arkle Beck. After 400 m (¼ mile) take the 1st road L by a walled garden. (**For link** to Route 4 continue on B6270)

2 Climb steeply to the end of the tarmac lane, then follow the track in the same direction, continuing to climb across the face of the escarpment. Near the top of the climb bear R on the main track and pass through gate in stone wall onto a flatter section

3 Superb views, in amongst mining spoils and heather. At T-j with lane by a farm R then at the junction by the telephone box bear L downhill

4 After 2 km (1¼ miles) go through gate and descend to cross stream over a small stone bridge. Soon after the bridge next L uphill on track towards then past farmhouse. At a fork of tracks at the end of the wall on the right bear L (in effect SA)

5 Follow the main track, climbing gently. Go past a standing stone dated 1867. At X-roads of tracks L around the rim above the top of the various stream valleys cut into the hillsides

6 Go past low wooden cabin, continuing on the main track through the mining spoils. At T-j by a stone wall with valley views ahead turn L

7 At T-j with a red metal gate ahead L alongside wall 'Footpath' then afer 140 m (150 yd) turn R to exit corner of field via wooden bridlegate

8 Bear R for 46 m (50 yd) to join better track. Follow bridleway signs along the LH edge of field. Exit field via metal gate and at fork of grassy tracks by the wooden fenced installation of Yorkshire Water bear R and follow this track as it swings L and descends steeply

9 At T-j with road R. Fast descent to Langthwaite.

10 Opposite the Red Lion PH turn L then bear R to follow alongside river. **NB** The middle section of the bridleway from

Langthwaite to Fremington, although beautiful, is narrow and bouldery, as much a push as a ride. For an easier alternative, continue through Langthwaite then at T-j with more major road turn L 'Reeth' to return to start

11 The rubbly section improves. At fork bear L on upper track then shortly turn R downhill towards farm 'Fremington 2¾'. Through farm and across fields following bridleway signs

12 Bear L steeply uphill by isolated stone house following the blue arrows. The next section will be slow as the track is narrow and bouldery

13 Track eventually improves. At T-j with road R downhill into Fremington. At T-j with B6270 R to return to Reeth

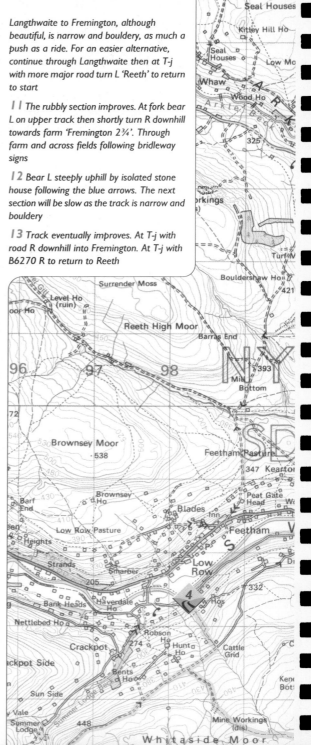

4 Along Swaledale and over Apedale

The second of two rides starting from Reeth, this one can in turn be linked to the Castle Bolton route, as they both share the middle section over Apedale. The route crosses the River Swale at Grinton then turns west, first on a road then on a bridleway, alongside the river which may be rough in parts although very beautiful. A better track takes you as far as Low Houses Farm which marks the start of the longest climb of the day, across the lane linking Swaledale with Wensleydale and up among the old spoil heaps on the top of Apedale. Care should be taken in route-finding on the plateau section as there are several other old mining tracks. A second climb from the crossroads of tracks by farm buildings up onto the top of Greets Hill leads to a well-drained, grassy descent that links to the Redmire-Grinton road and continues steeply down into Swaledale.

Start

The square in Reeth, on the B6270, 19 km (12 miles) west of Richmond

P As above (please contribute to honesty boxes)

Distance and grade

22 km (14 miles)
🌢🌢🌢🌢 Moderate/strenuous

Terrain

Riverside track, stone tracks through mining spoils and moorland. Two main climbs: 350 m (1150 ft) from Low House Farm to the top of Apedale Head; 130 m (430 ft) from instruction 10 to Greets Hill. Lowest

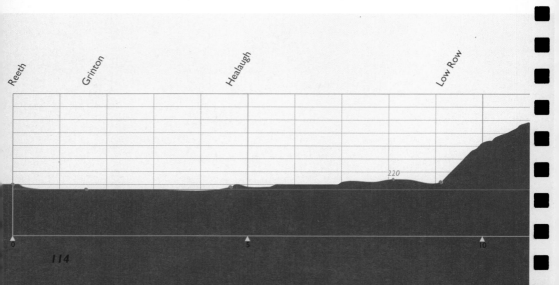

point – 175 m (580 ft) at the River Swale in Grinton. Highest point – 550 m (1800 ft) at the top of Apedale Head

Nearest railway

Garsdale Head, 32 km (20 miles) west of Reeth

Places of interest

Grinton 1 *(just off the route)*
The dead from outlying areas were once brought in wicker biers along the 'corpse way' to the Norman Church of St Andrew's, nicknamed 'Cathedral of the Dales'

Refreshments

Black Bull PH 🍺, *Kings Arms* 🍺, *plenty of choice in* **Reeth** *Bridge Inn*, **Grinton**

◄ Grinton

Whitaside Moor | Apedale Head | Apedale | Greets Hill | Harkerside Moor

550 · 430 · 510 · 550 · 180

15 · 20 · 22

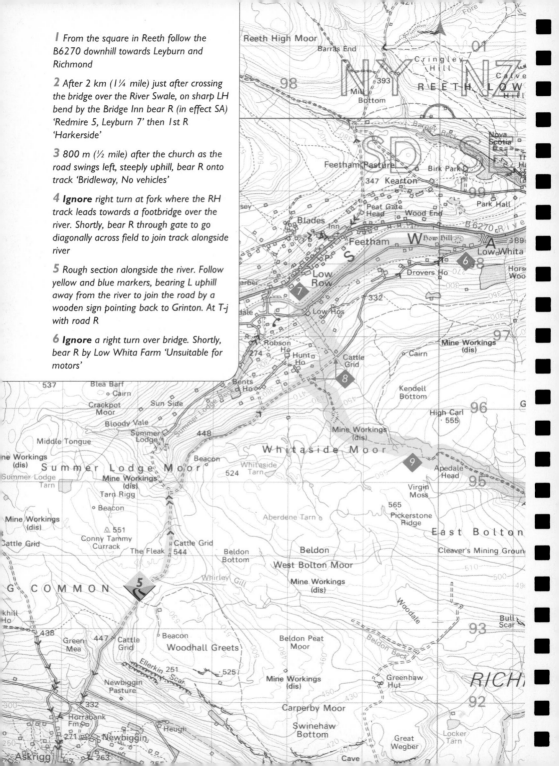

1 *From the square in Reeth follow the B6270 downhill towards Leyburn and Richmond*

2 *After 2 km (1¼ mile) just after crossing the bridge over the River Swale, on sharp LH bend by the Bridge Inn bear R (in effect SA) 'Redmire 5, Leyburn 7' then 1st R 'Harkerside'*

3 *800 m (½ mile) after the church as the road swings left, steeply uphill, bear R onto track 'Bridleway, No vehicles'*

4 *Ignore right turn at fork where the RH track leads towards a footbridge over the river. Shortly, bear R through gate to go diagonally across field to join track alongside river*

5 *Rough section alongside the river. Follow yellow and blue markers, bearing L uphill away from the river to join the road by a wooden sign pointing back to Grinton. At T-j with road R*

6 *Ignore a right turn over bridge. Shortly, bear R by Low Whita Farm 'Unsuitable for motors'*

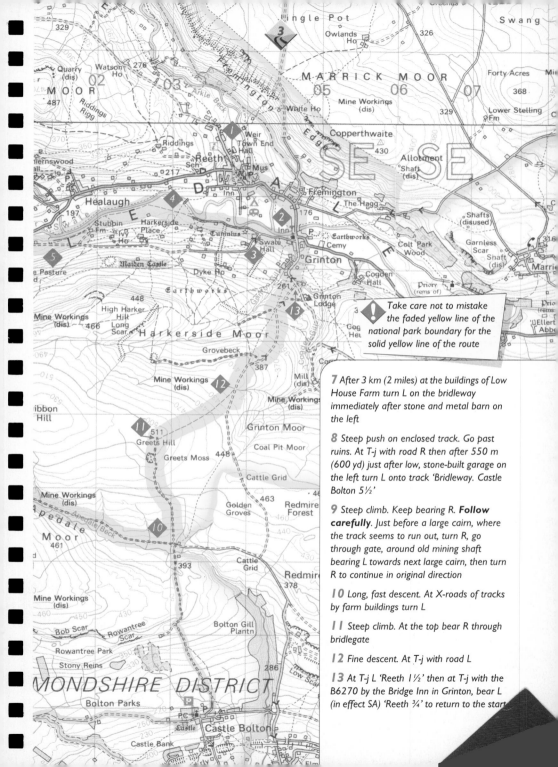

Take care not to mistake the faded yellow line of the national park boundary for the solid yellow line of the route

7 After 3 km (2 miles) at the buildings of Low House Farm turn L on the bridleway immediately after stone and metal barn on the left

8 Steep push on enclosed track. Go past ruins. At T-j with road R then after 550 m (600 yd) just after low, stone-built garage on the left turn L onto track 'Bridleway. Castle Bolton 5½'

9 Steep climb. Keep bearing R. **Follow carefully**. Just before a large cairn, where the track seems to run out, turn R, go through gate, around old mining shaft bearing L towards next large cairn, then turn R to continue in original direction

10 Long, fast descent. At X-roads of tracks by farm buildings turn L

11 Steep climb. At the top bear R through bridlegate

12 Fine descent. At T-j with road L

13 At T-j L 'Reeth 1½' then at T-j with the B6270 by the Bridge Inn in Grinton, bear L (in effect SA) 'Reeth ¾' to return to the start

5 North from Castle Bolton and up over The Fleak

Castle Bolton stands dramatically on the hillside above Wensleydale. The ride starts with a stiff climb on a track leading up onto moorland, joining a better track at the top of the hill. From the crossroads a good stone-based track is followed through Apedale, with one tricky piece of navigation near the summit. The descent provides plenty of thrills as you pick the best line down to the road where the day's third climb awaits you. 150 m (500 ft) of ascent on this tiny lane takes you to the top of the hill known as 'The Fleak'. Magnificent views open up ahead but your more immediate concern is not to miss the turning off the fast descent onto the bridleway that leads eastwards, back to Castle Bolton.

Start

Castle Bolton, 16 km (10 miles) southwest of Richmond

P Car park behind the castle

Distance and grade

24 km (15 miles)

Strenuous

Terrain

Mixture of grassy, rough tracks and good, stone-based tracks over moorland, old mining areas and farmland. Three main climbs: 180 m (590 ft) north from the start; 170 m (560 ft) west to Apedale Head; 150 m (500 ft) along the road to The Fleak. Lowest point – 240 m (790 ft) at the start. Highest point – 550 m (1800 ft) at Apedale Head

►*The view north from Hunt House*

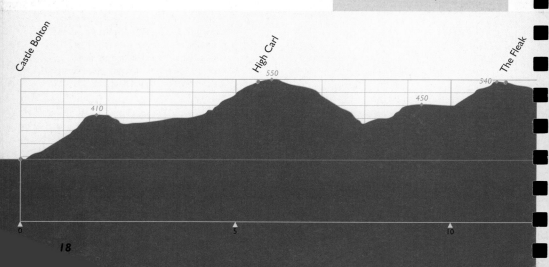

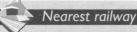
Nearest railway

Garsdale Head, 19 km (12 miles) west of the route near Askrigg

Places of interest

Castle Bolton /
Stone cottages line the rough green along the village's single street. The castle was built as a fortified manor in the 14th century by Richard Scrope, Lord Chancellor of England. Close by the castle walls is St Oswald's Church, also 14th century and built of pale local stone

Refreshments

Cafe at the castle, **Castle Bolton** *(seasonal)*
The following are all just off the route:
Wheatsheaf PH *,* **Carperby**
Kings Arms *, Bolton Arms,* **Redmire**
Crown Inn, Kings Arms *, tea shops,* **Askrigg**

Heugh

350

310

550

15   20

1 With back to the castle take the road towards Redmire and Reeth. After 46 m (50 yd) just before the telephone box turn L onto stone track between houses 'Bridleway. Low Row 6½, Grinton 5'

2 Short, bouldery push. Exit via gate onto moorland and bear L towards copse of trees

3 Long grassy climb. At the top of the climb go through gate onto better track, ignoring a left turn

4 At X-roads of tracks by the farm buildings at the bottom of hill turn L

5 Follow in the same direction climbing 170 m (550 ft) over 4 km (2½ miles) to a large cairn of stones 91 m (100 yd) before a fence running acros the hillside ahead. **Follow carefully**. Bear L at the cairn, follow the track round to the R by a disused mining shaft, go through gate, bear R towards a second large cairn then turn L (to continue in the same direction as instructions 4/5)

6 Keep bearing L across the old mining area. At T-j with road after fast descent L

7 Climb for 3 km (2 miles) then start descending. **Easy to miss** – after 2 km (1½ miles) of fast descent, take the 1st wide track to the L 'Bridleway, Castle Bolton 5¾'

8 Through several gates and one short, muddy section. After 4 km (2½ miles) as the main track swings right downhill towards houses, turn L at the end of a field through a metal gate onto a continuation of the line of the original track. Walled section

9 Go past mine workings, continuing in the same direction on a grassy track. At a gate with 'Farm Boundary' sign, the grassy track swings R then L, maintaining its height

10 At T-j with better track which heads downhill towards a small stone barn, turn sharply L uphill then shortly fork R 'Castle Bolton 2'

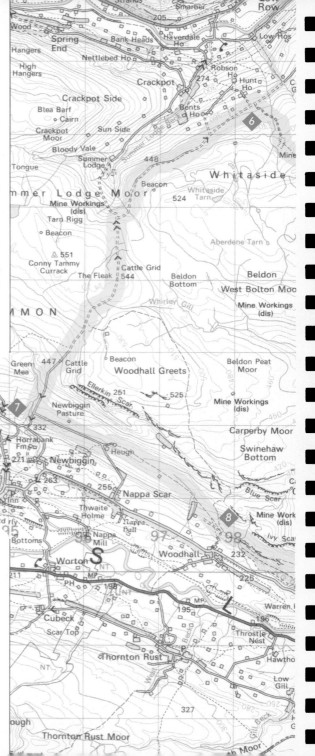

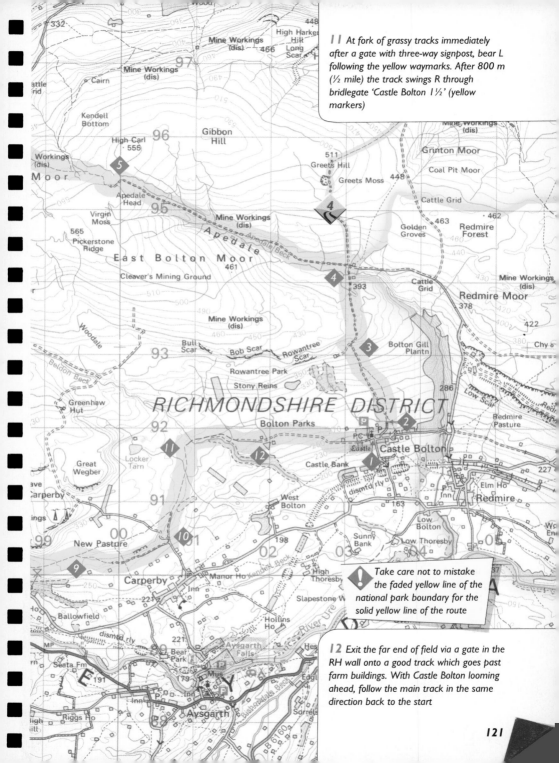

11 At fork of grassy tracks immediately after a gate with three-way signpost, bear L following the yellow waymarks. After 800 m (½ mile) the track swings R through bridlegate 'Castle Bolton 1½' (yellow markers)

Take care not to mistake the faded yellow line of the national park boundary for the solid yellow line of the route

12 Exit the far end of field via a gate in the RH wall onto a good track which goes past farm buildings. With Castle Bolton looming ahead, follow the main track in the same direction back to the start

From Aysgarth along Wensleydale and onto Stake Allotments

The A684, the only 'A' road through the heart of the Yorkshire Dales, is soon left behind as you follow the parallel lane through the hamlet of Thornton Rust to

▲ Aysgarth Falls

Start

The car park by the National Park Centre near Aysgarth Falls (signposted off the A684 Northallerton-Sedbergh road)

P As above

Distance and grade

24 km (15 miles)
🐚🐚🐚🐚 Moderate/strenuous

Terrain

Good stone tracks; a short, grassy section where route finding may be difficult; open moorland. One main climb: 280 m (920 ft) from Cubeck to the top of Stake Allotments. Lowest point – 180 m (590 ft) at Aysgarth Falls. Highest point – 540 m (1770 ft) at the highpoint on Stake Allotments

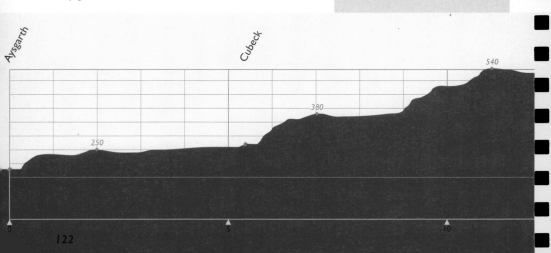

Nearest railway

Garsdale Head, 21 km (13 miles) west of the route at instruction 3

Places of interest

Aysgarth 1

Wensleydale is the broadest and most fertile of the Yorkshire valleys. It is watered by the River Ure, which rises on the western slope of Lunds Fell, 24 km (15 miles) west of Aysgarth. Near the village the rivers tumbles over limestone terraces in a series of three falls, known as Aysgarth Force. The best view of Upper Force is from the 16th-century bridge spanning the Ure. A footpath along the north bank of the river leads to Middle Force, and a little further downstream is Lower Force, the most spectacular of the three

Refreshments

George & Dragon PH ✿, Palmer Flatt Hotel ✿, tearooms, **Aysgarth** Crown Inn, Kings Arms ✿✿, tea shops, **Askrigg** (just off the route) George PH ✿, **Thoralby**

Cubeck where a steep, stony track leads southwest out of Wensleydale. A No Through Road is joined and followed south to its end as it turns to track. The moorland plateau is reached and the turn, off the main stone track, does not look at all promising – a bridleway sign points across an expanse of grassy bumps. The first 800-m (½-mile) section is by far the worst and soon a more visible track is joined leading for several kilometres towards the steep and distinctive, northern slopes of Penhill. The track becomes stone-based and descends steeply to Thoralby and the only refreshments *en route*. A last, short, steep road climb takes you back into Aysgarth.

Side Well

290

210

15

20

24

5

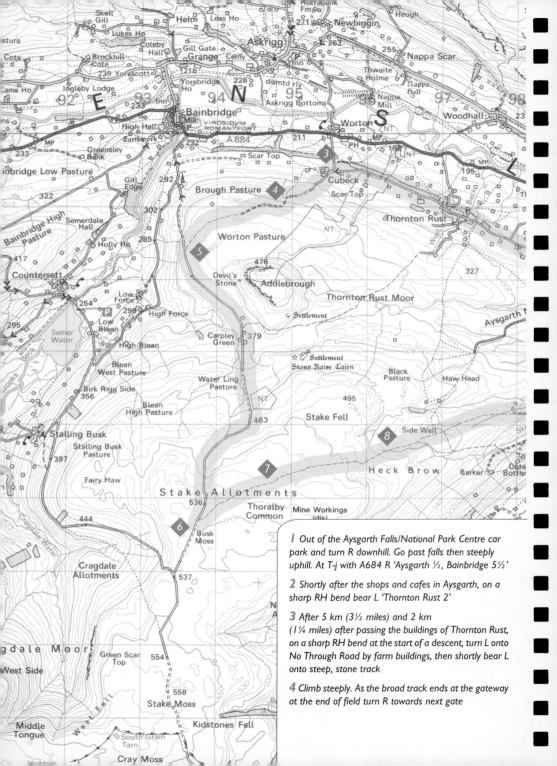

1 Out of the Aysgarth Falls/National Park Centre car park and turn R downhill. Go past falls then steeply uphill. At T-j with A684 R 'Aysgarth ½, Bainbridge 5½'

2 Shortly after the shops and cafes in Aysgarth, on a sharp RH bend bear L 'Thornton Rust 2'

3 After 5 km (3½ miles) and 2 km (1¼ miles) after passing the buildings of Thornton Rust, on a sharp RH bend at the start of a descent, turn L onto No Through Road by farm buildings, then shortly bear L onto steep, stone track

4 Climb steeply. As the broad track ends at the gateway at the end of field turn R towards next gate

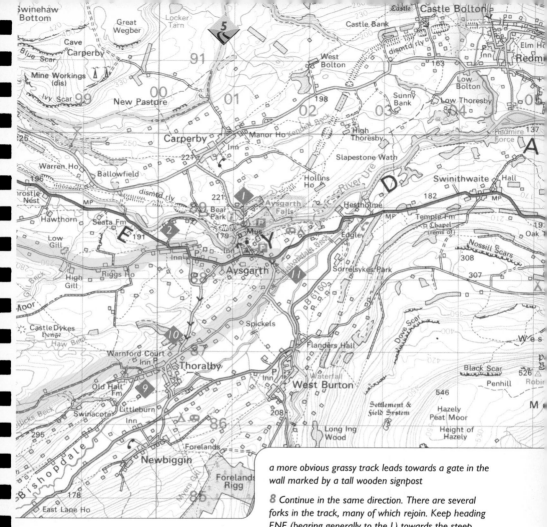

5 Continue in same direction on flattish grassy track through several gates, aiming towards the telegraph poles. At T-j with the road L

6 The road turns to track at the farm.
Easy to miss – 3 km (2 miles) after the farm, on a flat section shortly after passing a cairn on a hillock to the left, turn sharp L at the signpost just before gate 'Bridleway, Thoralby 4¼'

7 The route over the next 4 km (2½ miles) is at times vague and certainly much easier in good visibility. The first 800-m (½-mile) section is the worst. Cross the bumpy moorland, aiming towards the cairn, from where

a more obvious grassy track leads towards a gate in the wall marked by a tall wooden signpost

8 Continue in the same direction. There are several forks in the track, many of which rejoin. Keep heading ENE (bearing generally to the L) towards the steep 'nose' of the escarpment in the distance, passing a two-way bridleway sign and a small tarn on the left

9 The track is ever more obvious. Long descent. At T-j with road in Thoralby, turn L past George Inn. At T-j with more major road by the Post Office bear L 'Aysgarth 1¼, Hawes 10'

10 On a sharp LH bend 365 m (400 yd) after the Post Office bear R onto a narrow tarmac lane

11 At T-j at the end of the narrow lane L. At T-j with the A684 at the top of a short, steep climb turn L 'Aysgarth ¾, Hawes 10', then 1st R 'Aysgarth Falls Car Park' to return to the start

7 Down the Pennine Way south of Hawes

There are almost 10 km (6 miles) on-road at the start of the ride, following the river downstream to Bainbridge before cutting sharply back into the fells on the old Roman road that used to link the fort at Bainbridge with Ingleton. The climb is sustained but, almost all, rideable with ever wider views opening up behind, back down into Wensleydale. The plateau is reached and followed for several kilometres on track then tarmac lane. The route along the Pennine Way starts with an undulating section but the gradient soon steepens and the surface becomes quite rough in places. The track improves and you glide down via the back lanes of Gayle to return to Hawes.

Start

The Bulls Head Hotel, in the centre of Hawes, on the A684 between Sedbergh and Northallerton

P Follow signs at either end of Hawes

Distance and grade

32 km (20 miles)

🗡🗡🗡🗡🗡 Strenuous

Terrain

Good stone-based tracks over moorland. One rough and rubbly section on the descent. One main climb of 380 m (1250 ft) from Bainbridge to the top of the Roman road. Lowest point – 210 m (690 feet) at the crossing of the River Ure. Highest point – 590 m (1940 ft) at the top of Wether Fell

Refreshments

Crown PH 🍽, plenty of choice in **Hawes**
Rose & Crown PH, **Bainbridge**

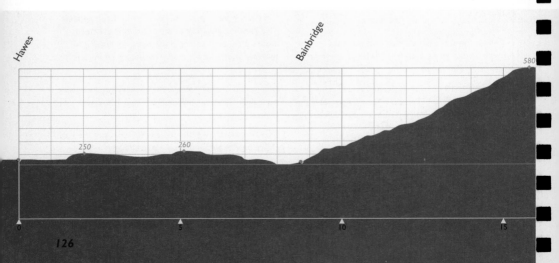

Places of interest

Bainbridge 4

In the Middle Ages the heavily wooded country to the south of the River Ure was known as the Forest and Manor of

Bainbridge and the village grew up around the spacious green which still has its stocks, grazing sheep and a profusion of daffodils in spring. The earliest inhabitants were foresters, who founded a custom that is continued to this day. Each autumn and winter night a villager takes a great bull horn off the wall of the Rose & Crown PH, steps outside and blows it, as his predecessors have done for 700 years. On a calm night its bellow can be heard several kilometres away, indicating the road home to lost foresters, through forests that have long since gone

◄ Hawes

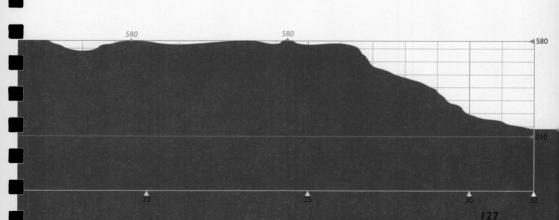

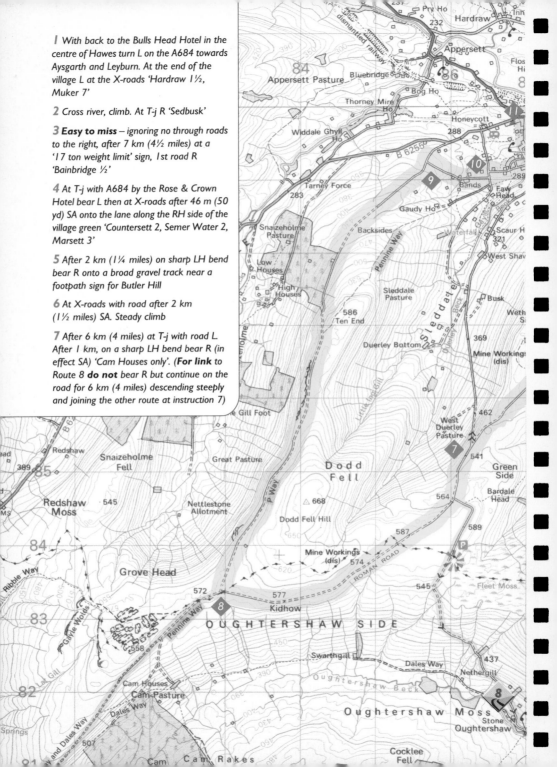

1 With back to the Bulls Head Hotel in the centre of Hawes turn L on the A684 towards Aysgarth and Leyburn. At the end of the village L at the X-roads 'Hardraw 1½, Muker 7'

2 Cross river, climb. At T-j R 'Sedbusk'

3 **Easy to miss** – ignoring no through roads to the right, after 7 km (4½ miles) at a '17 ton weight limit' sign, 1st road R 'Bainbridge ½'

4 At T-j with A684 by the Rose & Crown Hotel bear L then at X-roads after 46 m (50 yd) SA onto the lane along the RH side of the village green 'Countersett 2, Semer Water 2, Marsett 3'

5 After 2 km (1¼ miles) on sharp LH bend bear R onto a broad gravel track near a footpath sign for Butler Hill

6 At X-roads with road after 2 km (1½ miles) SA. Steady climb

7 After 6 km (4 miles) at T-j with road L. After 1 km, on a sharp LH bend bear R (in effect SA) 'Cam Houses only'. (**For link** to Route 8 **do not** bear R but continue on the road for 6 km (4 miles) descending steeply and joining the other route at instruction 7)

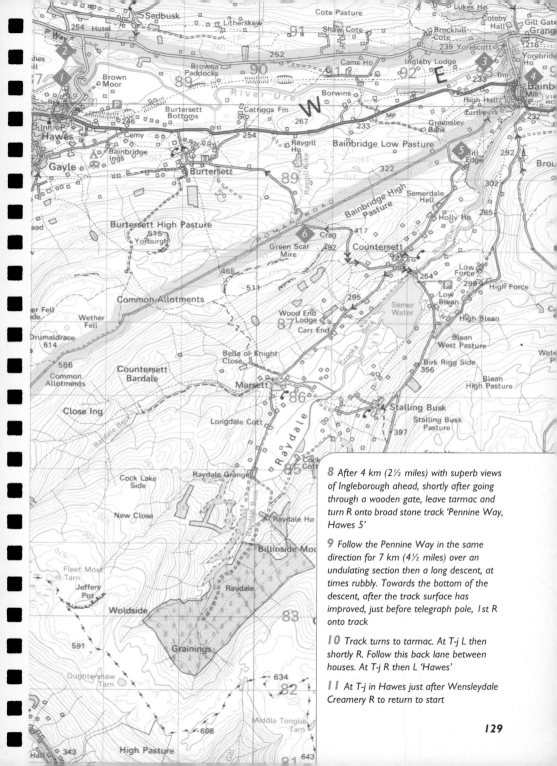

8 After 4 km (2½ miles) with superb views of Ingleborough ahead, shortly after going through a wooden gate, leave tarmac and turn R onto broad stone track 'Pennine Way, Hawes 5'

9 Follow the Pennine Way in the same direction for 7 km (4½ miles) over an undulating section then a long descent, at times rubbly. Towards the bottom of the descent, after the track surface has improved, just before telegraph pole, 1st R onto track

10 Track turns to tarmac. At T-j L then shortly R. Follow this back lane between houses. At T-j R then L 'Hawes'

11 At T-j in Hawes just after Wensleydale Creamery R to return to start

129

8 The Pennine Way, north of Horton in Ribblesdale

The ride follows a quiet lane to its end and continues climbing off-road past the delightful, wooded gorge at Ling Gill on the Pennine Way. The major junction of the Dales Way and the Pennine Way is followed by a rough section that has been severely damaged by 4-wheel drive vehicles. Shortly after joining the tarmac lane you have the option of linking with Route 7 and continuing along the Pennine Way into Hawes to make the ride into a much longer 60-km (36-mile) loop. From the plateau the road is followed steeply down into Langstrothdale before cutting west along the valley formed by Green Fell Beck, through the forest and along Birkwith Moor before the final, fast descent to Horton in Ribblesdale.

Start

The car park in Horton in Ribblesdale on the B6479 north of Settle

P As above

Distance and grade

35 km (22 miles)

////// Moderate/ strenuous

Terrain

Quiet lanes and stone tracks up onto moorland. One rough section northeast of Dales Way/Pennine Way junction. Two climbs: 320 m (1055 ft) from Horton to the restart of tarmac above Cam Houses; 80 m (265 ft) from Beckermonds to Birkwith Moor. Lowest point – 240 m (790 ft) at the start. Highest point – 590 m (1930 ft) over Bardale Head

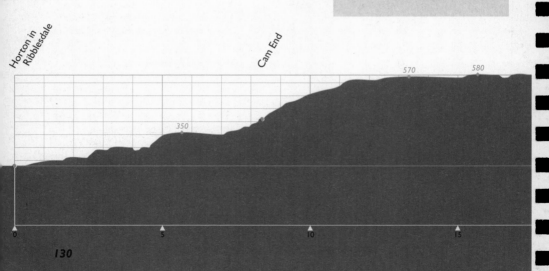